HR Like a Boss

HR LIKE A BOSS

Your Guide to
Amazingly Awesome HR

John Bernatovicz

Society for Human Resource Management
Alexandria, Virginia
www.shrm.org

Strategic Human Resource Management India
Mumbai, India
www.shrmindia.org

Society for Human Resource Management, Middle East and Africa Office
Dubai, UAE
www.shrm.org/pages/mena.aspx

SHRM books and products are available on most online bookstores and through the SHRMStore at shrmstore.org.

SHRM creates better workplaces where employers and employees thrive together. As the voice of all things work, workers, and the workplace, SHRM is the foremost expert, convener, and thought leader on issues impacting today's evolving workplaces. With nearly 325,000 members in 165 countries, SHRM impacts the lives of more than 235 million workers and families globally. Learn more at SHRM.org.

Library of Congress Cataloging-in-Publication Data
Names: Bernatovicz, John, author.
Title: HR like a boss : your guide to amazingly awesome HR / John Bernatovicz.
Description: Alexandria, VA : Society for Human Resource Management, [2023]
    | Includes bibliographical references and index. | Summary: "Human resources
    (HR) is the most important function within a business and this book strives to
    prove it. HR professionals are encouraged to focus on doing their best to have
    a positive impact on the people and organizations they serve"—Provided by
    publisher.
Identifiers: LCCN 2023011366 (print) | LCCN 2023011367 (ebook) | ISBN
    9781586444419 (trade paperback) | ISBN 9781586444464 (pdf) | ISBN
    9781586444518 (epub) | ISBN 9781586444556 (kindle edition)
Subjects: LCSH: Personnel management. | Organizational behavior.
Classification: LCC HF5549 .B4487 2023 (print) | LCC HF5549 (ebook) |
    DDC 658.3--dc23/eng/20230308

Printed in the United States of America   FIRST EDITION

PB Publishing

10 9 8 7 6 5 4 3 2 1

To the beloved memory of my mom and dad.

Contents

PART I
INTRODUCTION TO *HR LIKE A BOSS*

PART II
THINK DIFFERENTLY

PART III
BE DIFFERENT

List of Figures and Tables

Acknowledgments

The African proverb of unknown origin that states, "It takes a village to raise a child" relates to the feeling of what it took for me to author this book. The following people had a big part in making *HR Like a Boss* a reality.

A heartfelt thanks to my loving parents, Mike and Fredreen, for being the origins and biggest supporters of my creative and business aspirations.

A none-of-this-would-be-possible-without-you thanks to my wife, Emily; son, Will; and daughter, Mallory, for putting up with me talking about this book all of the time and allowing me to sacrifice time with the family to write.

A luckiest-guy-in-the-world thank you to my siblings, Tony Bernatovicz, Terese Gavin, and Andy Bernatovicz, for being so awesome and always being there for me in everything that I do.

An enthusiastic thank you to Bridgette Klein for encouraging me to write this book and being its #1 fan.

A cross-your-Ts and dot-your-Is thanks to the editorial support from Doug Adams, Jennifer Forgac, Karen Pupo, and Lori Weinstein.

An ARC (advanced reader copy) posse thanks to Ron Smith, Carly Bernatovicz, Christine Peters, Katherine Edgar, Lisa Mamula, Joseph Szafraniec, Andy Bernatovicz, Emily Bernatovicz, Nancy Flight, Tim Sackett, Katherine Valaitis, and Leslie Fouser.

An if-you-can-do-it-so-can-I thanks to fellow authors Steve Browne, Tim Sackett, Kris Dunn, and Ben Eubanks for bravely penning their own tales and inspiring me in the process.

A thanks-for-taking-a-chance-on-a-kid-from-Akron round of applause to Diane DeRubertis, Jackie Valek, and Liz Lamping for allowing me to experiment with the *HR Like a Boss* content in presentation form at KSU, NOHRC, and PHRA.

An everybody-needs-a-good-attorney-friend-to-protect-your-assets-and-cover-the-other-word-that-starts-with-ass thanks to Melissa Nasson and Salvatore Sidoti.

A big thank you to Matt Davis and Montrese Hamilton from SHRM Books—especially Matt for putting his faith in me to advocate on my behalf to SHRM Books and allowing me to share this inspirational tale of amazingly awesome HR with the SHRM community and beyond.

A you-got-your-name-in-the-paper-for-a-really-good-reason thank you to every HR and business professional who made a positive impression by doing *HR Like a Boss* (before it was a thing) and got quoted in this book, including but not limited to Bridgette Klein, Christine Peters, Steve Browne, Tim Sackett, George Sample, Amy Powers, Erick Miles, Lauren Rudman, Nickie DiCarlo, Jimmy Logue, Cindy Torres Essell, Marty Guastella, Todd Baughman, Dr. Melissa Briggs-Phillips, Jennifer McClure, Tana Mann Easton, Brian Rolnick-Fox, Brad Owens, Dave Ames, Claire Stroh, Lou Adler, Pat Tourigny, Tacy Byham, Kathy Sullivan, Michelle Leedy, Patti Stumpp, Dani Kimble, Philip Major, Steve Harris, Joseph Szafraniec, Ben Eubanks, Matt Soful, Kris Dunn, Scott Stone, Jenn Forgac, Chris Schmitt, Eda Erkal, Jeff Berquist, Wendy Worthington, Talia Seals, Cara North, and Zoe Switzer.

Finally, thank you to all of the HR and business professionals whom I have met over the years who inspired me to write this book and transform the standard of HR to be amazingly awesome!

Foreword

Change.

We toss about that word easily. Whenever it is uttered, we can experience a multitude of emotions. If we're honest, the word "change" brings about more anxiety and dread than it does a flush of positive emotions. This is particularly true when it comes to most human resources professionals. HR pros state they're comfortable with change when that is rarely the case. You see this through behavior far more than you do with aspirational words.

Now, please understand something. I am an HR professional. I make this statement because I was reluctant to change for the first half of my career as I felt I couldn't impact the business in any significant way. I had followed the example of others who had been in the profession before me. For decades HR has been expected to stay in its place. Unfortunately, we haven't pushed back against this expectation. It was far safer to stay on the sidelines and step in when, and if, we had to. Companies seemed satisfied with that.

Those days are gone. In fact, they've been gone for several years. We just haven't stepped out into the light. Senior leadership in organizations has been yearning for HR to provide more of a direct, intentional business impact. We remain stagnant and stuck. We're as frustrated as anyone else. It doesn't feel good to be overlooked, left out, and only engaged when there is a "people problem." It doesn't have to be this way. We don't have to be professionals eternally positioned on the sidelines. We can . . . change.

John Bernatovicz has captured and developed a tangible method to make this change a reality. If we take more ownership of who we are and what we do like a "boss," then we move from the sidelines to the heart of our company. He does a great job of painting a picture of where HR tends to reside and gives us direction, advice, and solid examples of what being a boss who practices HR looks like. It's not a matter of supervision. It's a matter of leading from your HR role.

This works. John is on point. I know this because he has done a masterful job of talking to HR pros who have embraced an *HR Like a Boss* mentality. They are effective examples of how HR is the vibrant, vital, and essential core of every company. The type of HR leadership John frames is enticing and exciting!!

Take the time to read, savor, and enjoy John's book. Then, be different and make a commitment to break with tradition. Blaze a new path where you can grow personally and professionally. Make the changes needed to move from a passive support function to an active leadership businessperson. It's worth the investment. Trust me. You'll love practicing HR . . . like a boss.

—Steve Browne, SHRM-SCP
Chief People Officer, LaRosa's Inc.
Author of *HR on Purpose!!*,
HR Rising!!, and
HR Unleashed!!

Part I
Introduction to
HR Like a Boss

Introduction

What am I doing?

After a long, tiring, and stressful day dealing with one employee issue after another, have you found yourself questioning your career choice? At that moment, I wonder if you have ever reflected and asked . . .

"What compelled me to get into HR in the first place?"

Like many others, I am sure your response to that question sounds like . . .

"I like working with people."

"I am looking to make a difference."

"I want to help people."

"I like to solve problems."

Do you think anyone in the history of the world ever answered that same question with . . .

"I like to fire people."

"I want people to be afraid of me when I walk into a room."

"I like to deal with paperwork."

"I want to do something that involves me making sure people follow the rules."

Here you are like countless other HR professionals who are grappling with the euphoria of what HR was supposed to be versus the reality of what it has turned into.

These questions and the endless possibilities of answers bring me back to a moment that showcased the gap between what HR *is* and what it *could be*. It happened during a presentation I gave to a local SHRM chapter amid the global pandemic. As I entered the room where they held the in-person meeting, there was a different vibe from what I experienced in previous presentations. Because of the abundance of caution and the various safety protocols put in place, this was the first time that I had given an in-person presentation in nearly eighteen months. Normally, when I walk into a room to present to a group of HR pros, there is a ton of energy, excitement, and enthusiasm. That was not the case this time around.

I chalked it up to the cold, dreary day and continued with my setup. Then, it came time to present. To get a read on the room, I opened my presentation with a question that I stole from Dr. Marc Brackett: "How are you feeling?" The response I received from the group took me by surprise.

Silence.

Not one person responded to my question. Over fifty HR professionals sat in silence.

I was not about to start my presentation like that, so I asked again, made eye contact with individuals, and encouraged the group to share their feelings.

One brave soul shouted out, "Tired." That was all we needed for the next five minutes. People shared their frustration about their emotions in dealing with what their role in HR had become.

It Hurts Sometimes

It was tough to hear firsthand from so many professionals—many of whom I admire—but I was not surprised. We've reached a breaking point. Nearly two-thirds of employees are not engaged at work, more workers are quitting their jobs than ever before, and almost every non-HR executive does not see the value of HR. Add in the unprecedented impact of COVID-19 on every single employee and employer in the world, and HR feels the hurt.

There is a gap between what it is and what I envision HR to be. That's what compelled me to write this book.

Why Do HR After All?

From head to toe and everywhere in between, I believe HR has the potential to be the most influential department in any organization. Regretfully, in too many cases it has been relegated to party planning and reductions in force.

We're here to change the way corporations and employees see HR. My sole aspiration for writing this book is to positively impact HR and swing the tide on how HR is done and viewed by all: an overhaul, a teardown, a 180, or whatever turnaround buzzword of the week that you would like to choose.

The HR that I see is leading every organization to be a purpose-driven company and is a permanent fixture at the leadership level. Executives, managers, and employees are running toward the HR that I see looking for help, guidance, and advice versus questioning why a meeting invitation was extended to HR. The days of "Am I getting fired?" are no longer. Instead, people will ask, "How am I being inspired?" when HR enters the room.

Every HR professional will be a savvy business leader first who just so happens to have an immense level of expertise in their selected HR discipline. HR leaders will drive business results by helping the organization align everyone around its strategy and long- and short-term goals while supporting its employees to reach their professional *and* personal aspirations.

HR will ensure organizations have a clearly defined and simple purpose with a community benefactor while hiring and developing employees that align with the core values and the culture of the business.

How will you do this?

This book outlines the five key elements of what it takes to do *HR Like a Boss*:

1. Think differently
2. Be different
3. Be better
4. Take action
5. Make an impact

The book provides specific suggestions and recommendations on how to transform the way the HR profession leads in the future and how all other employees look at HR.

A Little Bit about JB

Over the last few years, I have gone through a personal transformation of my own, all of which contributed to me writing this book. Being an author has been on my bucket list for years, and seeing some of my close friends, Steve Browne, Kris Dunn, Tim Sackett, and Ben Eubanks, successfully publish books sparked some unique motivation.

Then, I went through a tough stretch in my personal life, losing both of my parents in less than thirteen months. My mom was my creative inspiration, and I will never find someone who loved me more than her. She passed away on her terms on March 1, 2019. A few months later, my dad was diagnosed with terminal cancer, and he accepted my invitation to live with us so we could take care of him. Those three months were the most challenging and rewarding days of my life. Taking care of my dad was a blessing in so many ways, and it provided a perspective I did not have before.

Having devoted my entire career to serving the HR profession and starting a firm solely focused on supporting the HR & payroll community, I believed I had a unique perspective and felt compelled to share my views on what it takes to do HR in an amazingly awesome way. With that inspiration, I received the final "push in the back" from Bridgette Klein, my firm's director of marketing. She felt that the HR and business community would be inspired by the subject matter of a presentation that we had worked on and shared with HR organizations several times called *HR Like a Boss*.

After making my goal of writing a book very public through social media, committing every weekend for over one year to writing at least one thousand words, and getting tons of support and great ideas from the HR community through the *HR Like a Boss* podcast, I had a plan to make the dream of being an author a reality.

What You Won't Find in This Book

HR Like a Boss is all about helping you become a better human being, businessperson, and HR professional. Despite what you might expect from other HR books, the contents in *HR Like a Boss* have extraordinarily little do with the traditional HR concepts. There will not be any step-by-step guides to ensure governmental compliance. Nor will you learn how to write a handbook, administer benefits open enrollment, complete a compensation survey, or any other HR-specific tactics in this book.

Let's Go!

I hope that you are compelled by one of the key concepts or ideas from this book and it inspires you to do something different or better for yourself and your career in HR. In turn, my dream is that your new idea or action makes a difference not only in your life but for someone you know, love, or work with. You deserve and are capable of that type of change. I believe and hope you do too!

Let's begin your journey to amazingly awesome human resources and doing *HR Like a Boss*. Along the way, I'd love to receive your feedback, your goals, and your questions. Email me at john@willory.com.

Warning

This Book Might Offend You . . . But People Hate HR

The business community has a perception about HR. Right or wrong, it exists.

At times, there is an undercurrent of dislike combined with a misunderstanding of how HR adds value to the business. I am sure you have felt it at some point. Maybe there is some truth, and sometimes perception is reality. The only way that HR is going to improve its relations with other departments and buck these perceptions of "What the hell does HR do?" is to dig into the issues, run toward their frustration, and not back away when someone makes a snide comment about you or what you do.

HR is the most important function within a business, and we are going to prove it!

To do so, we must first understand the haters and gain their perspective. Together, we will run toward making the tremendous impact that HR can have on its employees, business, and the community.

HR professionals' frustration about how others view them became very real for me in early 2019. The Northern Ohio HR Conference (NOHRC) asked me to speak with HR professionals about looking at the function from a businessperson's perspective and what leaders are looking for from an HR pro. Of course, as a businessperson myself who runs a staffing and consulting firm serving the HR & payroll disciplines, this was a topic I was excited to talk about with the community.

But when I took a step back and started talking with non-HR professionals about my outline for my slide deck, the perception became real as many businesspeople I spoke with did not like nor see the value of HR. They suggested that HR is a bunch of rule enforcers and party planners and is often the axman—a department you want to avoid because interactions with HR lead to getting fired.

As I began to put my presentation together, it felt critical to discuss people's frustrations about HR. We cannot get to where we want to be without acknowledging current circumstances. The premise of my opening remarks centered on the idea that before an HR employee could be accepted as a business leader, they needed to be honest with themselves about how their colleagues and fellow employees saw them.

Figure W–1. One of my early presentations on how to do *HR Like a Boss* included Willory's director of marketing, Bridgette Klein, showing up as a literal elephant in the room. Check out the complete presentation and inspiration for this book at https://youtu.be/g8eMklSsl6Y.

As I continued brainstorming about this topic, I found myself googling "Why do people hate HR?"

Whoa.

There were over 76 million results in less than a second, everything from long-form articles to memes to videos to social media posts. I had stumbled across something that was clearly not new. However, why were we not talking about it?

I felt compelled to start my presentation and discuss why people hate HR. I had to address the elephant in the room, literally and figuratively.

As a result, I approached the presentation with a lot of apprehension, never more than in the few seconds I clicked to the slide that read:

I HATE HR.

For a moment, over one hundred HR professionals were staring at me. Did I make a mistake? Was this too much of a risk? Who wants to talk about why people hate them?

What happened next shocked me.

One of my goals during any presentation is to have the crowd interact with the content and create lively sessions with a lot of give-and-take. So instead of flat-out telling my audience that people hate them, I flipped it on its head and asked, "Why do people hate HR?"

It was a real issue with my HR audience. Instead of blank stares, hands shot up while many skipped that formality and just started shouting out answers. I could feel my blood pressure decrease, and I was relieved to find that what I was saying wasn't controversial at all. All I did was create a safe space for people to share, an outlet that included the following sentiments expressed as to why people tend to "hate" HR:

» HR is seen as the policy police, rules enforcers, and fun killers.
» HR puts the company first, employees second.
» HR is inflexible and hard to work with.
» HR is a managerial scapegoat.

» HR is an irrelevant, non–revenue producing cost center.
» HR is big brother.
» HR is the home for "no."
» HR raised the cost of benefits.
» HR is untrustworthy.
» HR doesn't deliver value.
» HR fires people.
» HR is the messenger of bad news.

Does this sound familiar? It isn't fun to be hated, is it?

If I had not stopped taking answers, this one topic would have hijacked the entire hour. This was a real issue for HR professionals—an entire discipline feels estranged from organizations because of these sentiments. One woman shared her story to the point that it brought her to tears. I had struck a nerve, but what was I going to do with that?

This book attempts to answer that question and why you should be doing *HR Like a Boss.*

Your personal perspective on this subject is critical as it should motivate you to do something about it. However, the mountain you must climb to change perceptions of HR is long and winding.

The pop culture view of HR is not one of good people working on behalf of both employees and employers but one of comic buffoonery. Toby from the TV show *The Office* and movies like *Office Space* poke a great deal of fun at HR with jokes about "TPS reports" and other silly regulations.

People hate HR mainly based on pop culture, personal experience, and past perceptions, all of which you cannot change.

You can change your approach toward your employees, managers, and executive teams. Don't feel sorry for yourself because people don't like HR or whine about the fact that you do not have a seat at the table.

Instead, focus on doing your absolute best and positively impacting the people you serve. Now more than ever, HR needs to deliver value to the business. We need to connect employees to the business goals and values. This will require creativity, hard work, and persistence. Along the way, try to avoid focusing on the outcome and simplify your efforts to add value and help everyone you serve.

Just like the infamous 2016 SHRM.org piece by Dana Wilkie, "Do Your Employees Hate HR?" suggests, go beyond what was or may have been the classic job description of HR and take extraordinary steps to help valued, yet struggling, employees. Take those steps because you "love people" and understand the organization's greater good.[1]

The only way to change the business community and popular culture is one interaction at a time. These small steps end up making a big difference.

The time is now, and it all starts with owning and loving what you do!

1. Dana Wilkie, "Do Your Employees Hate HR?" SHRM, February 5, 2016, https://www.shrm.org/resourcesandtools/hr-topics/employee-relations/pages/hr-success-stories.aspx.

Chapter 1
Defining *HR Like a Boss*

Are you ready?
Remember this moment as the time that you began your personal transformation to amazingly awesome HR, the kind of human resources that you did not think was possible. It starts right here!

What a "Boss" Isn't

You might be asking yourself, "What's the meaning behind *HR Like a Boss*?" This book answers that question and tells the stories of real-life human resources professionals doing boss-like HR. Later in this chapter, I describe what *HR Like a Boss* means to me and how the definition evolved after talking with countless HR professionals about what it means to them.

Before getting into the use of the word "boss" as meant in this book's context, we must start with what a boss isn't. A "boss" here is not the term culturally defined as a person in charge of workers or an organization. A boss is not defined by a specific title such as CEO, president, organizational owner, people manager, or anyone who leads or manages employees or an employer. You do not need to have the words "chief," "(vice) president," "senior," or "manager" in your job title to be a boss as defined in this book.

On top of that, a boss is not a bossy person. No one likes bossy people, and even bossy people tend to despise themselves! True bosses do not need to hold power over those within the organization nor do so condescendingly.

Speaking of loathing, my stomach turns when team members introduce me to others as "my boss." Now, I do realize that my team members mean absolutely no disrespect whatsoever. My hope is that it's quite the contrary. I never intend to create a hierarchy where there is a feeling of segregation between leadership and subordinates. Yes, you find my name at the top of an organizational chart where people typically write "boss," but more important than my place on this chart is my responsibility to drive results while developing and encouraging my team. If I can achieve this simple goal, my team members will reach beyond their potential and find a place of personal achievement they never thought possible. My objective is to *lead*, not to be their boss.

Now that we know what my intention is *not* when speaking about a boss, let's move on to the book's objective: to help you achieve boss-like status. In the remainder of this chapter, I define the phrase "*HR Like a Boss*," break down the two primary mindsets that a boss must have, and address the two most common barriers to achieve *HR Like a Boss* status.

Let's Actually Define HR

Let's start with what human resources is (or should be). "Human Resources" as defined by the Cambridge Dictionary is not so inspiring. By the way, dictionaries used to be books and not just a URL. One of the most classic dictionaries makes HR look more boring than anything:

The department of an organization that deals with finding new employees, keeping records about all the organization's employees, and helping them with any problems.[1]

The Cambridge Dictionary definition of human resources describes a very straightforward function primarily responsible for hiring, firing, and keeping a company legally compliant. Maybe this is one reason HR has become so tactical—some define our role as a tactical one of compliance first and foremost.

Instead, I would invite you to consider the John Bernatovicz definition of human resources:

Connecting people with the purpose of their organization

My definition of HR repositions it as a strategic partner. Connecting people to an organization or business will require HR to develop creative programs and solutions to ensure the entire organization is connected and clearly focused on business goals.

Unfortunately, as we covered in the reasons people hate HR, often HR is either not connecting or not seen as connecting people with the organization. Someone that does *HR Like a Boss* is a connector, a force that gets everyone on the same page for the good of the company, your employees, the community, and all other stakeholders. For the purposes of this conversation, I use the following list to encompass stakeholders:

» The company,
» Employees,
» Customers,
» Shareholders,
» Suppliers,
» Community, and
» Regulatory agencies.

1. Cambridge Dictionary, s.v. "human resources (n.)," accessed April 4, 2023, https://dictionary.cambridge.org/us/dictionary/english/human-resources.

Your list might look a bit different depending on the unique situation of your organization. I recognize the complexities of individual companies and don't want to diminish any of these groups, but *HR Like a Boss* primarily focuses on the company, employees, and community.

As you can tell, I have some strong views on the word "boss." My ideas stem from my viewpoint of famous and everyday bosses whom I admire. Throughout this book, you will read real-life stories of bosses who live the principles and do what it takes to deliver world-class HR.

Anyone can be a boss or do boss-like things because of their skills, stories, opinions, or abilities. That is why the word "boss" is so boss.

As you consider the potential of being a boss, let's reflect and ask the challenging question, "Am I making an amazingly awesome impact on the employees, the company, and my community?"

If you cannot answer with an emphatic YES, then keep reading for the fundamentals, techniques, emotional insights, and suggestions to learn how to do *HR Like a Boss*. Once you finish the book or throughout your reading, please do not hesitate to email me questions, insights, and comments like "you were way off with that," or to just say hello via john@willory.com. Yes, it will be me, and I will answer your email. If you prefer social media, try me at https://www.linkedin.com/in/johnbernatovicz.

If you answered that same question with a resounding YES, I would love to hear from you as well. Please keep reading, as there might be some additional validation of what you are doing every day (and you already bought the book).

My Original "Boss"

Let's take a moment to imagine achieving so much success that the term "the boss" is given to you in sincere reverence. As a kid, my brother, Andy, was a massive fan of Bruce Springsteen, and he wore out Bruce's records by playing them nonstop. I always thought Bruce was so cool, and I loved how he could captivate a crowd with a guitar, his voice, and a story.

My lifelong appreciation of Bruce "The Boss" Springsteen confirmed the use of the word "boss" in the title of this book.

The first time I tried to correlate "like a Boss" to "The Boss," it flopped like one of my infamously bad dad jokes. My first presentation of *HR Like a Boss* was an extra credit lecture at the business school of Kent State University, my alma mater. I could not resist breaking out my favorite Bruce Springsteen playlist to blast as the students filed into the auditorium. As one who grew up idolizing his music, I was mortified to see the blank stares on my younger audience members' faces when classics like "Born to Run," "Glory Days," and "Rosalita" blared over the auditorium hall.

I thought I was going to be so cool.

Figure 1–1. Picture of my brother, Andy (right), and I from our childhood. Check out his "Like the Boss" special edition of the *HR Like a Boss* video series at https://www.youtube.com/watch?v=rP4K_qgwmdM.

I miscalculated that prediction.

Unexpectedly, my presentation began with a music history lesson. After I turned the music down, the Kent State University student Society for Human Resource Management (SHRM) association president eloquently introduced me while I quickly retooled my planned introduction. I started with, "Who knows the name of the artist that sang the songs that were playing when you walked in?" Around 90 percent of the students looked at me with those same blank stares before a few raised their hands. I was encouraged by the hands, but that didn't last long. I asked them one by one if they knew the artist. Several got it wrong until a timid student made my day by sheepishly guessing, "Bruce Springsteen?"

It appears that Justin Bieber and Beyoncé have brainwashed some people (much younger than me) into thinking that they invented music. In the eighties however, Bruce Springsteen was one of the most famous and successful rock 'n' roll performers.

The Boss commands a room, as shown in the Apple+ TV documentary *Bruce Springsteen's Letter to You* on his career and his role as the leader of the famous E. Street Band with an amazing musical supporting cast of Max Weinberg, Nils Lofgren, Steven Van Zandt, and the late Clarence Clemons. Consider the importance of a supporting cast to any great boss. Bruce Springsteen certainly can attest to the positive impact that the E. Street Band had on his career. Bruce showed another critical boss trait by evolving his career to stay relevant by playing to sold-out crowds at his long-running Broadway show, *Springsteen on Broadway*, where it was just him singing and telling stories. Take a moment to reflect on your "bandmates" and how they are helping you to make rockin' music.

Transforming HR seems to me like something Bruce would encourage and respect!

Just as it is difficult for legends to achieve greatness, being a boss is not easy in HR. "Awesomeness" in HR is an elusive, ever-evolving aspiration. After all, HR deals primarily with people who can make us look like a savant for hiring them and, shortly after that, do something that completely baffles the mind. Being great at HR also requires excellence in a lot of disciplines. It is not as simple as doing *one* thing really, really well. Reaching boss status is about doing *many* things really, really well. Later, we review the top characteristics of someone who does *HR Like a Boss.* You could skip ahead, but where's the fun in that? Being described as wonderful, impactful, incredible, awesome, or amazing by your peers takes a special and devoted person who has developed and honed their skills and techniques to deliver fantastic support to the business and the people who work in it.

"Like a" Is Like . . . Really . . . Like Important

It is tough to overuse the word "like" in a book and feel you're getting your point across without the perfect Spicoli (from *Fast Times at Ridgemont High*) inflection and the right pitch and tone. As I define the word "boss" in the context of this book, it is equally essential to dive into the use of the phrase "like a" before the word "boss" in the phrase "*HR Like a Boss.*" These two words put the appropriate intention and charge into the phrase. The preposition ("like") followed by an article ("a") precisely placed prior to the appropriate use of the word "boss" shines the light on a comparison to someone doing it right and earning their status of being "in charge."

If you look hard enough and resort to the Urban Dictionary, you will eventually find a clean, HR-friendly definition of the "like a boss" concept as "used to describe something that someone did as amazing or awesome."[2] Perfect, right?

"Like a Boss" is enduring. People gravitate toward it. You can use this phrase to describe pretty much anything done better than what's typical or even what's simply good. I interpreted the Slang Dictionary on Dictionary.com, "Like a Boss" definition as to execute

---

2. Urban Dictionary, s.v. "Like a boss," accessed April 14, 2023, https://www. urbandictionary.com/define.php?term=Like+a+boss.

on something with commanding presence or an extra flair. This can be applied, tongue in cheek, even to fairly mundane tasks. The first recorded reference to "out like a boss" was in the 1993 Ice Cube song "Really Doe."[3] Since then, the phrase was popularized by The Lonely Island with an endless number of uses, including "I grilled that burger *like a boss,*" "folded the laundry *like a boss,*" "moved a piece of furniture *like a boss,*" and so on.

The stark difference when saying *HR Like a Boss* is that human resources is not a mundane task. In fact, HR is one of the top business functions closely tied to determining success or failure within an organization, business, or community. Whether it is done right or wrong, HR impacts billions of people's lives. Doing *HR Like a Boss* is of paramount importance.

Are you already asking yourself the question, "Do I practice amazingly awesome HR?" I hope so. For now, let's hold that thought. I will break down the principles of amazingly awesome HR later.

We've Talked about a Lot of Definitions, so Let's Define *HR Like a Boss*

Before doing so, we must take a moment to rag on the Cambridge Dictionary for their definition of the term human resources.

Clearly, this respected publication did not counsel any actual HR professionals when drafting their corny definition. So we must remember the simple definition from the (made up) Bernatovicz Book of Definitions and define HR this way: connecting people with the purpose of their organization and vice versa.

Working through the meaning of the words that make up the phrase still does not make defining someone who does *HR Like a Boss* in a sentence easy or even elegant. Creating a definition was no small task because of the differing opinions on which priorities

---

3. Dictionary.com, s.v. "like a boss," accessed April 14, 2023, https://www. dictionary.com/e/slang/like-a-boss/.

to emphasize. Some may argue that narrowing them down is not entirely possible or necessary. To me, it's imperative to develop a clear, concise definition to put a line in the sand about what doing *HR Like a Boss* means. Due to the abundance of varying perspectives, defining the phrase was certainly a journey.

I receive a different answer every time I ask people the question, "How do you define someone that does *HR Like a Boss*?" The variety of answers has astonished me. However, I harvested some consistent nuggets of gold to develop a simple yet detailed characterization. Based upon all of those opinions and years of experience seeing HR done fantastically well and horribly wrong, here is my original definition, which morphed into an abbreviated explanation, and then a long-form interpretation of the phrase created to change work forever.

"A businessperson who just so happens to practice HR" turned into "a leader who connects people to their organization in an amazingly awesome way." That evolved into "a courageous business leader who consistently owns their HR responsibility of connecting people to their organization in an amazingly awesome way while making a positive impact on their employees, organization, and community."

Boss Words

To me, there are ten words in the long-form definition that are critical to defining *HR Like a Boss*. They are listed here along with my two cents on how they connect to being "like a boss":

» **Courageous**: Be brave and lead with transparency and courage.
» **Business (acumen)**: You must have a profound understanding of business as a concept and, more importantly, immerse yourself into the company, trade, or organization you are in and understand not only what it does but how it does it.

- » **Leader**: You must lead truly, not just boss people around. Simple as that.
- » **Consistent**: People must know what they are getting with you.
- » **Ownership**: The word entrepreneur fits here. I don't mean real estate, companies, or stocks (although for capitalists, these things are not terrible). Being a boss starts with being an owner. The more you own, the better. The more you own, the better your attitude, results, impact on people, leadership development, and so on gets.
- » **People person**: They are the reason we do what we do.
- » **Responsibility**: Don't point the finger at anyone else but you. Try it out. It is compelling.
- » **Amazing**: Displaying excellence while actively striving to be better.
- » **Awesome**: Standing out from the crowd.
- » **Impactful**: Having every individual you interact with say, "I am better because of knowing fill-in-the-blank-with-your-name."

Does this sound like a lot? Maybe it is too much. I understand that the concept of transforming *HR Like a Boss* is bold, broad, and aspirational. How *you* do *HR Like a Boss* is up to you, but remember, your ultimate goal is to connect people with the business in an amazingly awesome way.

My Company's HR Boss

As my firm's first director of people operations, Christine Peters, says,

> *Someone who does HR Like a Boss is entrepreneurial and is always looking for improvements and ways to innovate. A boss removes obstacles and finds employees and peers the resources they need. A boss is always willing to look at how to*

do something better or differently to make an impact. They have to be really focused on how to create a positive experience for employees.

In full disclosure, I am quite biased toward my firm's first director of people operations and her people philosophies. That said, Christine Peters's HR career did not get off to a conventional start. After growing up in a family of five in a suburb of Chicago, Illinois, Christine followed her passion for theater and dance. She was an aspiring actress in touring companies across the country. Christine loved theater performances and sacrificed a traditional career to chase her dream. She traveled by bus and stayed in cheap hotels in small towns to pursue her childhood fantasy.

After realizing that making a living and pursuing a theater career do not always go hand in hand, Christine shifted her focus to another passion, numbers. I bet you did not think that her career would take a turn toward her math degree, but it did, and she got a job in data management. Eventually, her curiosity brought her to HR through a master's degree from New York University. After her life-changing, year-long worldwide trip, she and her husband moved to Cleveland with their two young girls. More recently, they've embarked on a journey to introduce a global perspective into their lives.

After reading that, you might think being the first-ever director of people operations at an entrepreneurial HR and payroll staffing and consulting firm might be plain old boring. Quite the contrary. Christine explained to me why she is thriving in HR: "I love working in HR because it touches just about every part of the organization. I interact with people in all different roles, understand what they do, and help them take their job to the next level. How can I make our processes better? What are the pain points and barriers? I really love that."

Christine continued with a fictitious, but accurate, example: "When you look at two companies that make sneakers, they're both making sneakers but what might be the differentiator is the innovation, research, quality, speed, and service level that goes into the end product. That difference is all based on the people. If you're not hiring, developing, and retaining the best people, it will drastically impact your company and your bottom line. Being in HR is about having that kind of far reach in a company."

For years, Christine has worn multiple hats at Willory. She's directed our people operations, managed our consulting practice, and served clients directly on projects. Christine definitely represents someone doing *HR Like a Boss* as she's taken the time to analyze her roles and responsibilities—personally and professionally—to understand how she can best empower people. As a result, she has transitioned from directing two functions to focusing on growing our consulting business while she looks for life-changing experiences with her family. Her results speak for themselves, and it's great to watch her apply her *HR Like a Boss* skills to this part of our organization.

Chapter 2

The *HR Like a Boss* Table Stakes

Having defined *HR Like a Boss* and before getting into the fundamentals of boss-like HR, it is of utmost importance to ensure these two core characteristics (and they are not up for negotiation) are present in who you are as a human resources professional: ownership and love.

A Boss Owns "It"

When I say a boss owns it, the "it" means everything within your control and what can be impacted by you. This list of impactable items is empoweringly endless. To be a boss, you must have a mentality of owning everything within your control. A boss is willing to take full responsibility and ownership over their position in an organization, both written and implied. It involves an obligation to ensure everything you are about and responsible for is at its peak performance. A boss positively expands the atmosphere of responsibility to cast over as many people, departments, managers, executives, and organizational tenants as possible. A boss is not limited by what is in their written job description.

There is one main caveat that I must interject: people are people. You cannot control what people do, say, or think. When speaking with countless HR professionals, it's evident that it can be exhausting when we immerse ourselves in others' problems, challenges, issues, and the list goes on. As HR professionals, we must be careful with showing concern for the people we serve and work to not burn ourselves out by feeling compelled to take my suggestion of "own everything" literally. When dealing with people and their emotions, stories, and issues, work to be more empathetic rather than sympathetic. This is no small feat and will require using your emotions wisely to master owning your own stuff while ensuring your understanding of what is going on in others' lives. Sincere empathy results from doing all that you can to put yourself into the other person's shoes.

The next time you find yourself involved in an employee discipline issue, layoff, or performance improvement plan, take a moment to imagine yourself in that scenario.

To handle these types of situations with empathy, it is vital to listen intently and repeat back what you have heard. Firing people over group Zoom conversations or mass email will never be seen as empathetic because there's no chance for a sincere feedback loop. Listening with empathy is a superpower that takes years to develop, but the impact of doing it consistently is profound.

"It" in Action

One example of a perfect opportunity to express empathy and demonstrate your listening skills might be working with a manager dealing with an employee struggling to hit their performance metrics.

To address the employee's performance issue, start by owning how both parties got to this point and what you could have done to prevent it from happening in the first place. Look back to the hiring process, interview method, onboarding practice, job expectations, performance management, and other employee-centric training opportunities to understand what caused the situation.

Next, dig into how you can support the manager in this situation. Remember, put yourself in the shoes of that manager to truly understand how they are feeling.

Finally, treat the employee with dignity and respect no matter what the circumstance might be. It can be easy to make the situation personal as the employee may have a family they support or you might be invested in the relationship. My encouragement is to own your responsibility, use empathy when listening to the employee and manager, learn from those experiences, and install guardrails like regularly checking in and observing managers during employee meetings or performance reviews to prevent it from happening again.

The first thing you can own 100 percent of the time is your attitude and commitment to practicing HR in a highly emotionally intelligent way. Your attitude should ideally be optimistic with a touch of concern that you are not quite doing enough. It starts with your professional ability to be truly aware of, have command over, and appropriately express your emotions while managing your personality to see the forest through the trees. It's no small feat (and countless other books are written just for mindset and EQ), but when your mindset and EQ are right, your confident professionalism should have a healthy dose of humility. One of the most committed instructional design pros that I know, Cara North, reminded me of this with a LinkedIn post where she paraphrased Laird Hamilton's quote about making sure your biggest enemy doesn't live between your own two ears. It is both accurate and okay that we need that constant reminder of what is in our head and how to use it wisely versus letting it control us.

Any interaction you have with your CFO, procurement director, software developer, or "fill in the blank with a title" must be infused with this "can do, people first, I own my responsibility" mindset. Then, we must look at everyone at our company and in our community whom we can impact. Look for not just those in our department, but all of the lives you can positively touch every day. You must run toward every opportunity and even more so toward the challenges your world faces.

To that point, Steve Browne (the author of *HR on Purpose!!*, *HR Rising!!*, *HR Unleashed!!*, and the foreword to this book, and one of the most beloved HR executives on the planet) recently shared at a roundtable that HR professionals "should feel exhausted after every day." Our HR work takes a ton of mental, physical, and psychological energy, especially as you work through the daily challenges and run toward the opportunities your people and organizations face. Are you exhausted (in a good way) at the end of every day?

As suggested earlier, a boss is not only applicable to management responsibilities. It means everyone with career HR aspirations—from a nervous college freshman entering their first HR class to the seasoned pro recently promoted to an HR business partner to a director tasked with turning around a struggling business unit—has a responsibility for people. Someone doing *HR Like a Boss* has a figurative (but it would be awesome if it was real) "own it" tattoo on their sleeve and is a pragmatic problem-solver who doesn't accept the status quo.

You might be asking yourself, Why do we have to own everything? The simple answer is because you are in HR. Human resources is the only department placed directly between the employer and the employees within a company. Finding yourself in that place is not for the faint of heart. However, it provides an opportunity available to no other department: responsibility for both the people within and the entire organization.

Think about that for a second.

Every single employee and how they impact the organization is your responsibility. The only other person within your company that faces that same challenging but totally empowering position is your CEO . . . that's it. As HR sits in this tight squeeze between the company and its people, you are in a place to impact how a company sees and utilizes its employees. At the same time, it positively influences the lives and careers of millions of American workers. Why stop there? Bosses can seize on the opportunity to positively impact billions of global employees by making a difference with each and every one of them.

Why Is This So Important?

You cannot underestimate the importance of work in people's lives. Just think about it the next time you meet someone new. First, they will rattle off their name. After that, the conversation will continue with where they are from and *what they do*. A person's career is part of every working adult's identity. Let's not forget the amount of time we commit to working compared to spending time with our family and friends (especially during the workweek in the prime of our career).

Speaking of friends, George Sample, an *HR Like a Boss*'er who eloquently owns everything he does, knows not just what an HR professional should be but also what they should do in today's business environment. I have a deep respect for George. He is a baller, figuratively and literally, in that he has major game in HR and plays "hoops for breakfast" as many days a week as he can. When he is not breaking ankles at the local YMCA basketball court or dropping knowledge at work, George is a family man with great devotion to his wife and tireless commitment to his two girls.

As for work, George has developed a career focused on serving the public sector in Cleveland, Ohio, working at the regional sewer district (it is not a poopy place—I couldn't resist), county library system, and Federal Reserve Bank.

As an example of how he owns everything, George is known to dance. More specifically, dance with me in front of two hundred cheering HR pros, dressed up like Steven Tyler from Aerosmith. Since George was up for having a good time and always had command of the stage, I figured it made sense to rap like Jam Master

Jay. Of course, George was my perfect sidekick as we pumped up the crowd to the classic rap-rock hit, "Walk This Way."

Enough about my antics with George. His attitude and credibility in the HR space give significant credence when describing the behavior of a boss doing what they do in HR in an amazing way as "someone who takes ownership. There is no 'that's someone else's issue, that's someone else's problem'; they take ownership of ensuring their organization is positioned for success to the best of their ability at all times."

In George's opinion, a boss has an entrepreneurial feel. They can see the big picture, and when it isn't easy to see it, they find it. I am not advising that you walk around and literally boss people around. That would totally defeat the purpose. Instead, I'm suggesting that you act like the owner of a business—your business, whether that is the entire HR department or a tiny sliver of it like benefits administration. Consider looking at everything you do, the people you help, and your role in your organization as part of your own small business. You are the CEO, CFO, CMO, CIO, and even chief sandwich maker. Make it whatever you want it to be, but most importantly, make it your own.

Be an entrepreneur. Here we go again with another definition. An entrepreneur is widely considered as someone who starts their own business, especially when this involves seeing a new opportunity.

Besides the "own business" part of the previous statement, don't miss "seeing an opportunity" as it is profoundly important to the definition of an entrepreneur. Your opportunity is to own your chance to improve as a business professional, truly define your identity, make an impact, and kick butt at HR. You are reading this book, so I presume you are seeking ways to take your HR game to the next level.

What Are We Waiting For?

You do not have to start your own widget business (unless you want to), but instead begin to think and act like an entrepreneur. What does that mean? Take ownership of your role and the organization you serve. Step up and take the initiative. Instead of looking for reasons why something isn't realistically attainable, dig into the real issue, then find the means to attain it. Never stop until it is done. Do not accept anything other than a finished product that you are proud to put your name on because it impacts your people and your business.

Amy Powers, a client turned friend, shared a concept she helped design and implement that aligns with this "own it" mentality: dedicated people plans. Established several years ago, her organization's (a global manufacturer of cryogenic equipment) executive leadership, managers, and employees implemented a progressive, evolving, and constantly evaluated performance management system. One of their core mantras is to "find your way to yes," which speaks to the mindset that all human resources and business professionals should have when dealing with customers and employees.

In your organization, department, or role, you know where there are problems. Don't let them continue. Bosses fix issues in a methodical, collaborative, and great-for-everyone-involved kind of way! Most problems stem from poor communication or people failing to meet expectations. A boss must connect the dots between organizational goals and the resources allocated to solve problems.

Unfortunately, the HR discipline often rewards behaviors that are not altogether entrepreneurial. Attempts at being a boss are thwarted as many HR tactical exercises demand precision and discipline, not entrepreneurial creativity. Accuracy and originality aren't mutually exclusive, but we often reward promotions and advancement because of our ability to complete tasks at a high level. It's the Peter Principle for HR. The business world rewards us for a job we do incredibly well by giving us a job we're not necessarily prepared to do.

Being an HR boss means being a model for your fellow employees. Set an example in how you manage your career and chart out a vision for where you want to be and how you will get there. Doing so will help you gauge your skills and competencies for your current role along with looking two or three steps ahead. Only then can you evaluate the gaps and what skills you need to develop.

Why "Own It" Is Personal

After going through some self-reflection while pouring out my thoughts, insights, and feelings to write this book, I realized my affinity for the subject of professional ownership. My perspective comes from my diverse career experience working in corporate America as an employee, being in various partnerships within small businesses, and having sole ownership responsibilities at Willory.

When I started my career at Automatic Data Processing (ADP), I didn't realize the safety net of the corporate environment. Early in my career, my myopic view didn't include how other employees were performing. I focused on my responsibilities and cultural norms, limiting my organizational ownership.

After ADP, my career maturation has included several business partnerships with small, entrepreneurial companies. It was quite the change from being an employee at a publicly traded company to having a genuine interest in my company's financial performance.

Business 101

Things drastically changed when I decided to start Willory as a sole proprietorship, and I was the only "employee" for the first year. In 2010, my ownership set off on a meteoric rise as 100 percent of an owner's unique responsibilities instantly became apparent. Days after starting my firm, I faced a tough decision on a client matter. I vividly remember sitting in my home office (Willory has been 100 percent virtual since Day 1) perplexed about what to do. My corporate America and small business partnership instincts kicked in, and I started to recall my steps of trying to solve problems:

1. Assess,
2. Think,
3. Reassess,
4. Rethink,
5. Ask for help,
6. Think again, and
7. Decide.

As I worked through my process and mulled over my options, I reached the "ask for help" stage. There I was, alone in my office, without a manager, colleague, or business partner. On top of that, my firm was way too early to have a board of advisors. What do I do? How do I make this difficult decision?

I realized that the "ask for help" in corporate America was easy. There were so many resources available that you almost felt protected from making a decision, let alone a bad one. At the very least, a decision did not carry the weight of "this is all on my shoulders." I looked around my office, struggling to navigate this newly created vacuum of decision-making, and it suddenly dawned on me: there is no one to ask for help! This decision is on me and me alone. In that instant, my mascot and the first dog I have ever owned, Lucy, moaned from under my desk. I think the weight of

Figure 2–1. Willory's first "advisor," Lucy

the room changed, and as a part German shepherd, she picked up on the gravity. At that moment, I blurted, "Well, what do you think we should do, Lucy?" Months earlier, I'd convinced my wife with two kids under the age of three that everything would work out with my start-up business. And there I was, a grown man, asking my 8-year-old German shepherd mutt how to navigate through a difficult decision. It was a watershed moment for me in my business career as it represented a professional migration into the supreme and absolute responsibility of actual ownership.

I wrote this book to help you be distinct by being entrepreneurial, thinking differently as you take full responsibility for everything you do, and taking the appropriate action to achieve results for the people you serve and your organization. Being a boss doesn't stop once you get a seat at the table. It is way more than that. A boss does not only dominate the seat they have earned; they effectively leverage it in the process. For those with unwavering grit and determination, you can be the first HR leader to turn your seat at the table into the head of the table by earning the opportunity to run the company or at the very least flourish within your business.

This is the mindset I'm talking about. Do you think that is possible?

Well, why not? You just have to love it enough to achieve "like a boss" status.

What's Love Got to Do, Got to Do with It?

I am trying to keep you entertained with an appropriate amount of (eighties) pop culture references. I hope you are not like my daughter, who tells me that my "dad jokes" aren't funny. Don't worry, I'll keep trying. Especially when I have the chance to drop a Tina Turner reference—she is a boss!

The first principle of being a boss is to own it. The next is love.

Once again, we cannot take the English language too literally, especially here. It's okay if you do not feel comfortable with using the word "love" at work. It reminds me of when my team read *Getting Naked* by Patrick Lencioni to advance our consultation game, and Christine Peters blushed every time she had to say the title in front of our team. So, if you feel uncomfortable, insert the word "passion" wherever you see "love."

Digging into "what's love got to do" with *HR Like a Boss*, I remind myself of a discussion I had with Erick Miles, an HR leader in Columbus, Ohio, and one of the thirteen original speakers selected for the inaugural DisruptHR Columbus event (Erick was unable to join us for the first event, but I can't wait to see him on the DHR stage soon). I met Erick and the entire group of stellar HR leaders through the community established by this truly unique event. Although he was a (self-proclaimed) miserable failure as a call center professional, Erick found his purpose in his love for people and pursued a career in HR. One of his cornerstone principles in life and business is having resilience forged by an unwavering love for what you do—which in Erick's case is doing *HR Like a Boss*.

"You got to find what you love to do. If you are not passionate about what you do, it will not be sustainable. Because the moment something happens contrary to what you define as successful, you will not have the buoyancy, power, ability, zeal, information, insights, etc. to be able to power through the difficult seasons that are a part of the maturation of who you are supposed to evolve into as an HR leader," explained Erick. "An HR professional needs to have a genuine love for people regardless of our differences."

Differences exist within everyone's view of ideology, morals, and values. Erick continued to drive home the importance of loving what you do by saying, "This passion will help you in everything you do and become your driver to make an impact. When it is time to show up and do something for people, we need to come at it with care and concern for those that may be different. This genuine love for people helps with being in the people business. Without love, I am not sure from where your motivation comes. If you are not passionate about what you do, you have to figure out what is blocking that passion."

As we position the idea of love in the context of business, look no further than the renowned research project by Dr. Melissa Cardon that defined entrepreneurial passion as "consciously accessible, intense positive feelings experienced by engagement in entrepreneurial activities associated with roles that are meaningful and salient to the self-identity of the entrepreneur."[1]

The key to this statement and to having this type of love or passion goes back to taking an ownership mindset, which results in getting you where you need to be to achieve your goals. Frankly, I couldn't care less what you call yourself to get the right juices flowing to drive results and make an impact.

Hear me out on why this is so important. To make that impact and have the feverish desire to persevere through every oddball, harebrained, you-can't-make-this-stuff-up thing that people do and HR gets to deal with, you've "got to love" what you do.

While doing my research and speaking with hundreds of HR professionals to write this book, I started to wonder about the age-old story about why so many initially decided to pursue a profession in human resources. The common answer is, "I like working with people" or the ever-popular and wildly confusing, "I am a people person."

Who Cares If You Like Working with People?

Why does "liking to work with people" even matter? Liking to work with people is just the start. Frankly, some HR professionals end up becoming jaded by their experiences with people and ironically find themselves despising the same people that inspired them to choose HR as a profession in the first place. Instead of saying "Uh-oh, that

---

1. Melissa S. Cardon, "The Nature and Experience of Entrepreneurial Passion," *Academy of Management* 34, no. 3 (2009): 517, https://doi.org/10.5465/amr.2009.40633190.

stinks," this makes me think of only one thing: there is a tremendous *opportunity* here for those with an entrepreneurial, "own it" mindset.

For years, we have heard people say that they got into HR because "I like working with people." It sounds cliché, and it is not enough—we must go all in on the emotional scale to make a real impact. Many of the HR professionals I know who are amazingly awesome at HR genuinely love working with people. The HR profession is in the front row of the roller coaster ride of life at work, which provides us with an immense opportunity every day. Someone who does *HR Like a Boss* works tirelessly to ensure that the people they love (it is okay to say it) are getting the most out of their experience at work. It is not a romantic love in the traditional sense but more of a passion for making a difference. When you are pouring your heart into helping people become the best at what they do and how they support the company's purpose and goals, you'll be pointing them on a path that will advance their career and helping them to get the most out of the countless hours they spend at their jobs.

This is where I think it is totally (once again said in your best Spicoli voice) acceptable to use the word "love." We are not talking about loving just one person or your CEO. A boss loves helping every single human in their network achieve their personal and professional goals. Whether you are the sole HR professional for a hundred-person food distributor or one of a thousand HR professionals supporting a global empire, the chance to make an impression with your love for what you do (aligning people to drive results for your organization) is the opportunity of a lifetime.

Let's break down the math on this and make it realistic for you. *Workforce Analytics: A Critical Evaluation: How Organizational Staff Size Influences HR Metrics* suggests that on average across all companies involved in the survey, the median HR-to-employee ratio is 1.11:100. SHRM suggests that "the HR-to-employee ratio provides a more manageable way to compare HR staffing levels between organizations."[2] Many factors, including supporting technology (or its underutilization), scalable processes, and organization size will dramatically impact the HR-to-employee ratio.

For the sake of making the following point, we will use round numbers of 1:100. Let's dissect the math into small and attainable daily or weekly tasks that create meaningful habits for improving the service you provide to your employees. Imagine if each HR professional devoted two hours out of their week to build deeper relationships with the employees they are responsible for, got to know them, and supported the professional growth of their 100 employees. The impact on the employees, the organization, and that HR professional would be profound.

Hear me out.

If you hold hour-long meetings each week with two out of the 100 employees over one year, you will meet with every one of those employees in a disciplined yet informal way. Once in place, the managers consistently meet with their employees, and a human resources team member joins quarterly to ensure that people properly execute people's plans, check that development is taking place, address challenges, and recognize success. These scheduled meetings are in addition to effectively working the shop floor, catching up at the watercooler, doing a Zoom check-in, or hanging out with the sales department as part of your daily routine. Doing this will prevent that "oh no, HR is in the meeting, am I getting fired?" look in most employees' eyes when an HR professional enters a room.

By having an intention to develop relationships and doing so in a meaningful way, please consider one of my brief pontifications about love overcoming hate. Society has lost sight of this fact, and many feel compelled to be right while being overbearing with their

---

2. John Dooney, *Workforce Analytics: A Critical Evaluation: How Organizational Staff Size Influences HR Metrics,* Society for Human Resource Management, 2015, 2, https://www.shrm.org/resourcesandtools/business-solutions/documents/organizational%20staff%20size.pdf.

Table 2–1. When looking at the median, companies have roughly 1 HR professional for every 100 employees. How does your company compare?

HR-to-employee ratio	n	25th Percentile	Median	75th Percentile	Average
Overall	945	0.42	1.11	2.02	1.70
Small Organizations (2–99 employees)	254	1.72	2.65	4.51	3.66
Medium Organizations (100–499 employees)	295	0.78	1.19	1.70	1.30
Large Organizations (500–4,999 employees)	239	0.20	0.58	1.01	0.91
Extra Large Organizations (5,000+ employees)	157	0.01	0.07	0.56	0.48

opinions. Some take it a step further by bellowing about how anyone who disagrees with them is wrong.

Purposeful and caring relationships require love, and building them the right way takes time. You cannot cut corners. Each relationship will blossom over time and will be different for each person. However, people must feel that HR truly cares about them. It is the only way to have an impact, and bosses do that in spades.

What Can Get in a Boss's Way?

At times, human resources professionals have the ownership mentality and passion for people, but they still get stuck. If you aspire for more from your career, then you must remove the external barriers that are in your way.

Organizational structure and leadership are two common impediments that can get in your way.

Let's break down how your company's organizational structure can impede your boss-like status. Before leaving my first job with ADP (a *Fortune* 500 company), I realized that I was not going to be able to make meaningful changes in this large and highly profitable business because the processes and organizational structure had been developed over fifty years. At times, huge companies struggle to provide a culture of creativity and their environment feels more like a large cargo ship making its way across the Pacific Ocean. As soon as it leaves port, its course is set to reach the destination with few opportunities to stray off course or try something new. Many feel safer in a group-decision-making environment, where they attend meetings, reach a consensus, make decisions, and move forward. There is safety in feeling more comfortable in a setting where everyone shares responsibility. Consider yourself challenged to find a way to seize that entrepreneurial opportunity and break out of the norm. Take that risk!

Working with HR professionals, I have heard countless times how leadership will not buy into the impact that amazingly awesome human resources can have on the culture, bottom line, growth, and productivity of the organization. It is a real thing, and this fact was one of my inspirations for writing this book. Why do leaders of organizations feel this way about HR? If you face a CEO, CFO, or another executive leader within your company who does not see the impact of great HR, you must, *you must* dig in.

First, make sure that you build relationships so you can afford the space to ask tough questions. Do so with vulnerability and ensure that you hear the words, emotions, and nuisances that are shared with you. You cannot be afraid of the answers given, and you must lean into what you hear. In turn, your relationship with that person will blossom as sprinkles of trust are formed. I see countless HR professionals talk themselves out of having the difficult conversations necessary to align leadership and advance your people and organization. For those executives with predisposed notions about how HR has been in the past, it is your responsibility to prove to them through careful planning, strategic thinking, precise execution, positive cultural impacts, and engaged and productive people that HR does make a difference.

Additionally, leaders tell themselves stories about what they think about HR and why they haven't invested in leveraging all the resources available within a well-run HR department. As part of your rebranded HR plan, you must understand their perspective. Once you gain their viewpoint and break through the barriers, then the fun stuff is ahead, including

» strategic planning;
» purpose, mission, or values alignment;
» employee feedback;
» effective performance management;
» realistic and useful succession planning;
» impactful talent acquisition; and
» leveraged talent development.

All of these should be a stable fixture in your leadership discussions in order to most effectively align your people with the right jobs to drive sustained profitable growth and results. Instead of blaming the leaders who are preventing you from implementing your ideal HR organization, take ownership to assess, learn, empathize, strategize, and plan. Then, execute a people-first HR strategy that engages your employees and drives results for your business.

It takes this type of focus to deliver amazingly awesome human resources. Someone who does *HR Like a Boss* wants and needs to be responsible for everything and removes barriers to reach the desired outcomes. Once you have earned the trust of your leadership team, you must be willing to take a risk and stick your neck out. You might be wrong or make a mistake, but you must learn to be okay with that. A boss is not just *willing* to make decisions solely and live with the consequences; they *thrive* on that pressure. Yes, not every attempt will go in, and every decision will not be infallible. A boss pushes forward rather than letting the fear of a wrong decision or taking a risk stop them. A boss collects information, data, and opinions and is willing to make an informed decision. A boss knows that the most significant mistake an individual or organization can make is not deciding at all. Mistakes happen and cannot be avoided with consensus. Learn from the process of making that decision, then own and learn from the result (no matter the outcome).

Lauren Rudman, a confidant of mine and kick-ass HR executive, agrees that leading *HR Like a Boss* takes courage. She defines someone practicing *HR Like a Boss* as a "fierce business leader who is self-aware, not afraid to make a decision, and a great collaborator and connector within the organization."

If you do not know Lauren Rudman, you should find a way to connect with her. Lauren is a force of nature in the HR community. I had the pleasure to sit on a board that she led for the local Cleveland SHRM chapter, during which she was an early adopter of the DisruptHR concept and a proponent of bringing it to Northeast Ohio. This was way before DisruptHR was a household name in the human resources community. She also played a crucial role in galvanizing the giving aspect of HR professionals' devoted organization by formalizing Cleveland SHRM's charitable foundation.

Like Lauren, someone doing *HR Like a Boss* understands the barriers within their business, culture, and people and runs toward the issues that exist. Do not let the organizational structure, negative perceptions of HR, or haters of what you do get in your way of your pursuit of delivering amazingly awesome HR to your team, employees, and organization. You will get to the root issue holding back your people and your business.

Are You Capable of Doing *HR Like a Boss*?

Of course, you are! It all starts with owning what you do and having an immense passion for people and business. As you embark on the rest of this book, consider Erick Miles's eloquent challenge about loving what you do and ensuring your professional purpose aligns with your personal aspirations.

Doing *HR Like a Boss* begins by asking yourself some tough questions:

» Do I genuinely love working with people, and am I passionate about helping them?
» Do I run toward making an impact on people and my organization?
» Do I love the idea of business?
» Do I believe in the leader of my company?
» Do my beliefs align with what my company stands for?
» Do I truly understand how my company makes money?

Complex questions with crucial answers. Before we start on the journey of amazingly awesome HR, you must begin with your purpose and ensure you are "all in." It is okay if this is not for you. Really, it is.

I hope you're with me about why doing *HR Like a Boss* is so important and how it can help your career. *HR Like a Boss* is the mindset of a businessperson who just so happens to be practicing HR. They run their job, function, or department like a business and have an "own it" mentality. On top of that, bosses *love* what they do, and their passion exudes from their pores in everything they do. In the coming chapters I discuss the fundamentals of doing *HR Like a Boss* and what it takes to change your world by being boss-like.

Part II
Think Differently

Chapter 3
Thinking Is Paramount

In previous chapters, we defined amazingly awesome HR and the importance of having an ambitious mindset with the boss-like cornerstones of ownership and love. This chapter will dissect specific ways to think differently through strategizing, learning, and self-care to build the foundation for making an impact and seizing your opportunity as a human resources professional.

As we embark on this journey of thinking differently, I am reminded of the now famous five-year ad campaign in the nineties for what was, at that time, a struggling tech company: Apple. Today we consider the award-winning "Think Different" campaign brilliant, no matter how much criticism it originally garnered for its grammatical incorrectness. Defiantly, Steve Jobs and his ad team created a famous series of commercials on how leaders and creative thinkers "Think Different." None of whom, by the way, were using Apple products in the advertisements as the iPhone or Mac were not around during the heydays of Albert Einstein, Bob Dylan, Martin Luther King Jr., John Lennon, Thomas Edison, Muhammad Ali, Amelia Earhart, and Pablo Picasso.

The design of this ad campaign and ultimate organizational transformation successfully reframed Apple from a struggling company on the brink of bankruptcy to a visionary brand. Apple would use this campaign to launch a historic run and become one of the most successful publicly traded brands and companies in US history. Those who noticed and invested in Apple are likely experiencing financial freedom that they could not imagine back in the late nineties. A $10,000 investment in Apple at the time of the release of the "Think Different" ad campaign would equal multiple millions of dollars in current market value. Basically, everyone in the world has a smartphone and Apple is part of the world's culture due to its innovation, community impact, and outstanding financial performance.

Are You Ready to "Think Different"?

Constantly evolving, learning, and growing are a huge part of taking ownership and being passionate about what you do. Taking time to think *differently*, and dare I say *better*, increases your potential of making a true impact on your organization and its employees. It's important to look within and assess the how and why of what we do before diving into the what. Take time to examine the deeper elements of success to transcend what you do with meaning and purpose. We must look at everything differently, and that all starts with you and how you find a better way for the what, how, and why of HR.

Carol Dweck writes about evolving, both professionally and personally, in her classic book *Growth Mindset*. She describes someone who cares about development as wanting to think differently, see the big picture, make an impact, and be responsible for others. She explicitly details the difference between a "fixed mindset" and thinking differently by aspiring for a better "growth mindset." She reviews how we look at and think about the simplest to most complex things, the effect our mentality has on how we deal with what happens around us, and our inner drive to change for the better.[1]

---

1. Carol S. Dweck, *Mindset: The New Psychology of Success* (New York: Ballantine Books, 2007).

Someone looking to improve and do *HR Like a Boss* is constantly aspiring to grow through every daily challenge. Dweck's growth mindset formula is

Growth = Effort + Coaching + Time

Applied together, she posits, this simple formula will help you improve and grow.[2] Put in the work, learn from those who have taken an interest in you and your career, and be patient as you develop through countless life lessons and experiences. If we were to expand upon the formula, I would highly recommend considering adding the variables of continuous expansion of knowledge, skills, and expertise.

To transform your organization and impact the employees you serve, look at how you approach the HR discipline and ask yourself, "Am I serving the business or the tactics?" Someone transforming *HR Like a Boss* goes beyond traditional HR and its necessary but tactical functions to make an impact. They do so by aligning the organization's most critical resource, its employees, with its business goals. Don't misunderstand me: tactics and compliance-related matters are essential and must obviously be done correctly. However, focusing on tactics limits your ability to impact the business and puts you in a (nonstrategic) box. Keeping your organization off the radar of the alphabet soup of regulatory bodies like DOL, IRS, EEOC, and ADA, is critical, but don't stop there. Don't let doing it cost you your strategic, boss side.

Compliance is (obviously) essential, but it cannot be the only component of HR you focus all your attention on. As several guests on my podcast have alluded to, it can take two different mindsets to adequately manage the compliance and strategy sides of HR. Because of this, it might even make sense to look to separate the two activities. Someone thinking differently will follow compliance, but someone must be championing HR strategy too.

2. Dweck, *Mindset.*

A cornerstone strategy of doing *HR Like a Boss* is putting your people before everything else, even including profitability when necessary. Putting people before profit should not be done in a vacuum as you cannot lose sight of the obligation your organization has to its shareholders. It must be an organizational commitment from all stakeholders. As a result, it's never wise to make short-term decisions like cost-cutting measures to ensure a certain stock price or hitting your quarterly estimates that, in the long run, destroy your long-term strategic focus and differentiator, an unwavering commitment to your people. Do not forget the long-term impacts on your culture, values, customers, and purpose when you sell your soul and put profits before people.

Ultimately, it is up to you to think differently about *everything you do* because taking a people before profit mindset is a core job responsibility of doing *HR Like a Boss*. It is also up to you to work tirelessly to convince everyone in your company, even your numbers-driven, bottom-line-focused CFO, to take a long-term view and consider the financial implications your people have on the business, your customers, and the community. It's easy to get caught up in the short-term, compliance-focused, survive or be killed, profitability at all cost way of thinking. But there is a reason why many prudent investors use a strategy that invests in companies set up for long-term success and why organizations author articles about and have entire practices devoted to purpose.

To that point, Peter Fisk wrote in his 2019 LinkedIn article "Why Do Purpose-Driven Companies Do Better?" that "purpose-driven companies are more ambitious, attract the best talent, inspire richer innovation, make faster decisions, are more trusted, have greater loyalty, and attract more investment."[3] His article also stated that "purposeful companies outperform the stock market by 42%."

---

3. Peter Fisk, "Why Do Purpose-Driven Companies Do Better?" LinkedIn, February 1, 2019, https://www.linkedin.com/pulse/why-do-purpose-driven-companies-better-peter-fisk.

If you're revolutionizing *HR Like a Boss,* you want to achieve these outcomes:

» Attract better talent,
» Increase innovation,
» Make quicker decisions,
» Build trust,
» Captivate loyal customers, and
» Continuously "ace" all measures of business performance.

Thinking differently by aligning your purpose to your employees, organization, and community makes an impact. Wendy Worthington, a well-respected HR leader and corporate HR executive in Cleveland, Ohio, stresses the importance of the tenet "alignment and collaboration between the employees and organization drives results for both parties." It takes that type of risk and different types of thinking to transform your employees, your company, your customers, your brand, your purpose, and your community.

Invest Time to Think Like a Boss

How much thinking do you do every day? Thinking is required with almost everything we do, but have you ever said to yourself, "I just need to focus on strategizing and big picture thinking"? Of course you have! The problem for many of us is that this tends to describe most of our days. We say it, but don't do it with discipline and rigorous attention. The wide array of distractions that get in your way set back your productivity. Activities like checking emails, responding to texts, falling into the office gossip, creeping on social media, masterminding fantasy football trades, and participating in the dreaded back-to-back-to-back meeting marathon can bog down even the most active professional. We end up getting stuck in the minutiae and focusing on what is immediately in front of us.

The only way you can make the change to stop and think strategically is to adjust your process and build a unique method or system for strategic thinking. In his book *Atomic Habits*, James Clear describes in detail how to create life-altering habits through tiny (as little as an atom) and repeatable changes to your behavior.[4]

One of Clear's brilliant suggestions is to associate or pair a new habit into an existing process or thing that you already do. As an example, if reading more is a habit you want to improve, try the following. Let's assume you eat breakfast every day. Try to pair up reading a book or blog or listening to Audible while scarfing down your Cheerios as part of your morning routine. This experience lasts about ten minutes or so per day. Ten minutes does not sound like a lot, but it is a significant accomplishment in forming a new habit. That's precisely the point—an atom is very small and so is the first step in creating a new habit.[5]

I myself took a recent self-improvement journey. When I began to write this book, my business coach suggested that my early struggles of getting the proper words on the page were due to "impostor syndrome." As I doubted my ability to author a book, she suggested exploring my fear of being a fraud. Then it dawned on me. How could I write a book when I do not even like to read myself? Digging into it further, I realized that I never liked to read even as a kid. It is a miracle that I got through, let alone performed well in school. I realized my sophomore year of college that buying new books at a premium and returning them at the end of the semester for pennies on the dollar was a bad deal for me and a great one for Dubois Book Store, the now defunct bookseller on the Kent State University campus.

In my junior year, I decided to save the money I received from my college golf scholarship allocated for books and use it for something more important like beer or pizza. So, in my junior and senior

---

4. James Clear, *Atomic Habits: Tiny Changes, Remarkable Results; An Easy & Proven Way to Build Good Habits & Break Bad Ones* (New York: Avery, 2018).
5. Clear, *Atomic Habits*.

years of college I did not buy one textbook because I knew I would never read them. Mind you, my college education was extremely worthwhile, mostly because I was one of the few college students who religiously went to class. That's how I learned: not by reading, but by going to class and listening to professors' lectures.

Fast-forward to now, when I found out by mistake (thanks to my mother-in-law's accidental Audible subscription) that I thoroughly enjoy consuming audiobooks and can do so at a 50:1 clip to sitting down and reading. I realized the best way to make this a habit was to pair my book listening time with something I was already doing. So, I started to listen to books while doing outside yard work and commuting in my car. Before discovering audiobooks, I habitually listened to my favorite music playlists while mowing the grass or spreading mulch in my yard and consumed local sports talk radio when driving in my car. Now I listen to books. In one year with this new habit, I read as many books as I had read in the prior forty years combined. Think about that—I implemented

Figure 3–1. Picture of me during my Kent State University years

a change in my habits by combining my desired growth in reading with my weekend-warrior yard work duties and windshield time in my car.

Plus, I no longer feel like a fraud and have a life-altering habit that will make me a better businessperson and human being.

It was also because of this experience that I was insistent with the editor that *HR Like a Boss* also be available as an audiobook. I know I'm not the only auditory learner.

Once I committed to this new habit, I worked tirelessly to avoid breaking the habit chain. This is a way to keep up the habit and not let anything stop you from pairing up reading a great article with your morning cup of joe, outside chores, or during your morning commute. You must repeat this every single day and never look back.

This stick-to-it-every-day mentality is vital as you will be tempted time and again by distractions. To avoid the distractions that get in the way of us doing some of our most important work, let's use a tool we tend to live by and in, Outlook or another email or calendar application. Start with a weekly appointment titled "think" on your calendar. Do not negotiate the time away and build a habit that will ensure you stick to it.

Using Clear's pairing trick to help me create a habit of strategic (detached from the universe) thinking while taking a stroll on a local park trail or getting in a few laps on my neighborhood cul-de-sac worked to perfection. I find that my best ideas come when I completely disconnect from everything, including my work, phone, and family (sorry Em, Will, Mal, and our puppies who love to tag along). So I intentionally take one or two walks per week devoted to just thinking about ways to improve my business.

This sense of getting away reminds me of the many conversations I've had with Nickie DiCarlo. Nickie is a one-of-a-kind friend, and her devotion to her family, work, and friendships is unparalleled. Nickie has extensive HR leadership experience with multiple manufacturing and financial services organizations, which prepared her to launch her HR consulting firm dedicated to helping organizations attract, develop, and engage top talent to meet strategic objectives.

Nickie shared that she blocks out 8–9 a.m., 12–1 p.m., and 4–5 p.m. on her shared calendar so that other people could not schedule her where they found white space. She filed this under "I am the boss of me" category. This time was reserved for her to use however she needed or desired. Sometimes that time was for her to schedule or decide to accept a meeting. It was often used to complete tasks. Additionally, one of the daily slots is used for a mental break, walking outside alone or with a friend.

As Nickie reflected, "I should have done more of it, because it definitely helped me come back refreshed—especially after occasions of having 'hit tilt.' My guess is it would be difficult to find a professional who spends most of their workday in an office who didn't also acknowledge the benefit of stepping away and/or getting out for a breath of fresh air to clear the mind."

Why is taking a pause so important? From my personal experience, there are a number of calming aspects, both physically and mentally, that come with slowing down. When we get lost in the monotony of the daily grind and the constant motion of action, we lose sight of ourselves, our well-being, and the bigger picture.

Slowing down and devoting time to thinking and strategy will allow you (and those around you) to work *on* your business instead of *in* your business. "Working in the business" is the physical act of doing things while "working on the business" is the act of strategically thinking about the what, how, who, when, and why of the things you do. To me, "working in the business" is attending meetings, conducting a candidate prescreen, administering a COBRA claim, writing a job description, and so on. It is the tasks that you do on the ground floor of work. "Working on the business" is taking a thirty-thousand-foot view of your business. It looks more at the why and the how, and then dissects what is discovered to find ways to improve, scale, and create efficiency.

Someone who does *HR Like a Boss* takes time to study and understand the business, the industry, and their discipline(s). It's a tactical method to think every day. For nonreaders like myself, other learning methods include resources from podcasts, social media, news apps, and websites.

What will you think about? Take time to learn about an important aspect of your company's business, either through your research or through scheduling time with people internally. This can and should include researching your industry or your respective discipline (HR leadership pieces). Whatever your process is—however you best think—take time daily to be a boss and think about solutions.

You may not be the boss in charge of the corporate organizational chart. However, you must take control of what you are responsible for, do the absolute best you can do in your role, and own the outcome no matter what it is. If you take the time to think and carefully strategize, you're well on your way to doing *HR Like a Boss.*

Don't Give Time or Mind Space for Reasons or Excuses

This chapter is all about maximizing the real estate value between your two ears. I have provided some suggestions on investing time in thinking, but the brain can often get stuck obsessing over emotions or feelings. These thoughts can consume you and distract even the most emotionally intelligent people. Have you ever been so sideways about a conversation or comment that you made that you find yourself thinking about it nonstop? You replay it repeatedly as you get ready for your day, shower, dress, brush your teeth, eat your cereal, drive to work, and so on. Should I continue? Well yes, I think I will.

I'm going to digress for a moment from the concept of mind space. It reminds me of when I fell in love with my wife. I was in my sophomore year of college and was living with Jimmy Logue, one of my great friends to this day. I was busy playing on the golf team, attending class, and trying to have a social life. I dated a few girls in college but always had my eye on this tall blonde from my hometown. She had gone off to college and was adjusting to life away from home. Occasionally, she would call me to share her concerns and how much she missed her family. After a few months of the calls, my soft-spoken, man-of-few-words roommate at the time says to me, "Man, Emily is calling you a lot. Do you think she likes you?" His question hit me like a bowling ball to the stomach. Once I proverbially picked myself off the ground, I realized that I might have a chance with her. For the next couple of months, I could not get my mind off of her and kept scheming ways to find time to spend with her. Eventually, we were able to connect, and Jimmy was right. The rest, for Mrs. Bernatovicz and me, is history.

This fall-in-love-can't-think-about-anything-else feeling is euphoric and for some, only something we experience once or twice in our lifetime. Just like when we fall in love, we can become consumed by or with thoughts about a decision we made, an email we read, the way the CEO addressed our team, or how a colleague looked at us while passing in the hallway. To me, time is so very precious. We cannot sacrifice our mind space with thoughts that slow us down or distract us from the ultimate prize of doing our job amazingly well. We're here to truly make an impact on our employees, business, and community.

Making an impact is vital as we drill into the mindset required to do *HR Like a Boss*. Later on, I dive into the importance of emotional intelligence. Almost all of the successful HR professionals I have been fortunate enough to know or do business with are educated in this area and hyperaware of their EQ. The science behind emotions is growing, and I am by no stretch an expert in this field. Unfortunately, the majority of our feelings and instincts have a negative slant to them.

Another barrier to being in the right headspace is that many do not address this nagging pest of regret or remorse. They attempt to shut it down or move on, but that little voice—just like in *Field of Dreams* (if you build it . . . they will come)—keeps persisting until you deal with whatever is consuming your thoughts.

Tick. Tick. Tick. Boom!

Many people have baggage and most of us try to avoid dealing with it until these deep-rooted thoughts rear their ugly head and impact our behavior when we are pushed into a corner or have a bad day. I recall a scene from the show *Cheers* where a lovable small-town guy, Woody, who transplanted into the big city tells psychiatrist Frasier that "I was raised to believe that if you have a problem, you lock it away in a secret place . . . you keep it bottled up, good and tight . . . and if it gets full in there, you just keep forcing the pain down and clamping it in."

In response, Frasier turns to a fellow bar patron and simply mimics a clock ticking.

Our partners, kids, team members, executives, and stakeholders may all have things that make them a ticking time bomb. We are all potentially in a position to think, "I've got something way deeper going on than I will ever let on, but push me too far and I may blow." Someone who does *HR Like a Boss* doesn't underestimate the amount of baggage that exists with those you love, work with, and support. Having an empathetic ear and genuinely trying to understand what is going on with whomever you are trying to support and love is paramount.

In the same way, acknowledge your baggage and deal with it separately. We could spend endless chapters on this subject, and quite frankly, I am not a psychiatrist. I don't even play one on TV nor have I recently stayed at a Holiday Inn Express, but there is an element to being mindful and sympathetic in the HR discipline. HR needs to give and receive information, much of it personal. Find a way to mitigate your own baggage through mediation, positive self-talk, mentorship, life coaching, counseling, or professional therapy.

I work on this myself daily, and one thing that gives me a slight head start is not filling my mind with reasons, excuses, doubt, regret, and negative storytelling. Those doing *HR Like a Boss* understand the importance of looking at hardships as challenges instead of problems. The stories that we tell ourselves are compelling. In many cases, the tone of these stories can justify our own perceived personal ineptness on fill-in-the-blank issue or cover up our inability to honestly deal with the problems we face. Therefore, we point our infamous index (appropriately also known as a pointer) finger around to the most accessible target, which is usually anyone or anything else that isn't ourselves.

Crucial Conversations (start at crucialconversations.com for the book and their resources) is a great resource that is complex but highly effective at dealing with our stories and how they impact our ability to navigate through conflict, tough discussions, or forward-thinking initiatives. Check it out to learn the steps to run toward tough conversations and free your mind for productive work and meaningful relationships.

To be able to navigate through everything you must deal with in the field of HR, you must be in a good place mentally, ready to receive, respond, and retool whatever comes your way. If not, you will suddenly find yourself using that pointer finger way too much at the expense of advancing your employees and organization to reach their potential and beyond.

Chapter 4

What Do Bosses Care About?

When I think about a great leader, I immediately think of an individual who cares about employees and their organization more than themself. They understand that to reach their individual goals they must set out to require a more extensive collective effort. You've heard the clichés: "The whole is greater than the sum of the parts," "There is no 'I' in team," and "We are only as strong as our weakest link." A cliché is a cliché for a reason! They might be overused and unoriginal, but in them exists truth. We hear a lot of coaches in sports, especially the good ones, take all the blame when the team loses but distribute the praise to their players when the team wins. Influential leaders understand this straightforward but counterintuitive way of thinking. To achieve the outcomes for your department, your organization, or in this case, *your* business, you must look from the outside in and figure out what motivates others for you to achieve your personal goals and aspirations.

A good leader should care about you and your results more than arriving at 8 a.m. sharp versus 8:02 a.m. It's likely that your favorite boss in your career was very clear on expectations and got out of the way for you to perform. Your best boss probably

»   helped you figure out a plan,
»   developed measurable metrics,
»   pointed you in the right direction,
»   tracked your progress with the metrics,
»   encouraged you when needed,
»   coached you when you needed help, and
»   cleared the path when barriers arose.

Several books are written about what we deem servant leadership. They're taking an "it's more about you versus me" approach. Servant leaders aspire to listen more than they talk, enjoy giving a gift more than receiving one, take great joy in seeing others succeed over their personal achievements, and so on. They focus on the growth of their team members as opposed to their selfish, personal gains. A servant leader gets that it is about their people, not them.

Having this approach is not only handy when dealing with conflict—it's critical. Often, people involved in a conflict are so caught up in the stories they tell themselves and why they are right and the other person is wrong. They cannot see how they are acting and its effect on those involved in the discussion or debate. By seeking to understand how something impacted the other person, you will defuse a potentially tension-filled situation while creating a connection with the people involved.

Get at the Spider

When you lead by example, colleagues, peers, executives, and friends will seek you out to help them manage a crisis or address an issue head-on. This positions you to make a difference (be a boss)

and fortify a personal connection to people in a way that you can only achieve by getting to the root cause, the spider, of an issue and persevering, together, through turmoil. Often, these spiders are very personal and have nothing to do with the reason the conflict exists. Most people in a business climate do not want to go that deep. They say, "This is business, it is not personal," and like the second agreement in Don Miguel Ruiz's bestseller, *The Four Agreements*, they "don't take anything personally."[1] I agree with that idea in theory, but it can be hard especially as many issues that exist in business can feel very personal.

Expand Your Thinking

Now, let's expand our approach to thinking differently one step further. Teach through examples those in your department, in other functions, managers, and your executive team to take on that "I get more joy from giving a gift than receiving one" mindset. Imagine an entire department, managerial team, or executive group focused on the goals, aspirations, and outcomes of others versus doing whatever it takes to achieve the results it needs. This will lead to more "what can I do to help the others" thinking, leading to teamwork and collaboration rather than the lonely and ineffective feelings of isolation. Leaders must take a "what is best for we, not me" mindset, avoiding the selfish and siloed approach that many employees and departments develop. With a selfless, greater-good mindset, HR can create and influence organizational and individual life-altering change.

As an HR professional, take the time to train employees on the finer points of being a boss. HR has a unique ability to impact company culture and encourage employees to take ownership, improve, and help grow the business through selfless, boss-like acts.

---

1. Don Miguel Ruiz, *The Four Agreements* (San Rafael, CA: Amber-Allen Publishing, 1997).

Study Your Company (The Who, What, How, and Why)

Maybe you have seen the popular reality TV show *Undercover Boss*. When studying your company, there is no need for those in the real world to dress up in disguises to really learn what is going on in their business. True leaders engage with employees at all levels and know the who, the what, and the how of their business. Whether you report to the president, the CEO, or an HR manager, get to know the products your company makes or the services your firm provides. I recommend starting with the frontline workers who deliver the primary function that generates revenue for your company.

Not-So-Undercover-Boss, Ohio Edition

During Cindy Torres Essell's first six months on the job as the HR leader at Heinen's Inc., she put on a uniform and went to work at their twenty-three gourmet grocery stores. Cindy is the first member of her family to earn a college degree, and she didn't stop there. After graduating from college, she went on to earn her Juris Doctor degree.

During her onboarding, Cindy took one day a week to visit stores and employees, as her leadership philosophy starts with being empathetic: "You can't be an HR leader and not understand the business."

She explained her approach as "learning and understanding the business is tremendously helpful because it enables you to have meaningful conversations with business leaders that you couldn't have if you didn't understand the business. More importantly, these conversations and understanding the business enable you to develop better solutions. You have to be a businessperson, not just an HR person."

Initially, it is of utmost importance to start with senior leadership. Understanding the CEO's vision for the company and how the purpose, core values, and culture aligns the people to this vision is critical. Ensuring the remaining senior leadership team's viewpoint parallels that of the CEO's is critical for organizational success. In the event there is a conflict or inconsistencies, it is imperative that you explore the where and why of the inconsistencies. Consider Cindy's "study your company" approach when getting to know your leaders, people, sites, and finances. As a result, Crain's Cleveland Business awarded Cindy and her team with its Excellence in HR award. This annual award recognized Heinen's for having the best HR department in the community.

At times, a lack of alignment exists primarily when things are unclear. It causes confusion and a lack of consistency with the company's direction and subsequently its employees. Understanding the why behind a leader's behavior is critical for your success in HR. We must take an active role, as HR is ultimately responsible for ensuring alignment of the organizational direction. Meanwhile, point every department and its employees in the same direction as their leader. Everyone has a piece to play in achieving the leader's vision, and it is HR's job to align the team with its leader(s).

While serving *HR Like a Boss*, your organizational understanding of visions should extend beyond your own respective leader to departmental leadership. It's your job to support every department—do you know what type of employees the vice president of marketing needs and wants? Do you know what the departmental priorities are for information technology? Whether there's a job requisition or not, whether there's a challenge or everything is running smoothly—get to know the departments you're partnering with and their goals.

With Bruce Springsteen's influence on the title of this book, it only makes sense to include Marty Guastella, SPHR, SHRM-SCP, lead singer for the rock 'n' roll cover band Ricky & The Rockets. If you are into the Beatles or want to see an HR leader rocking out, check them out at www.rrockets.com. A well-respected HR pro by day and singing front man by night, Marty knows what it takes to harmonize and get people singing from the same proverbial sheet of music. How does he do it? One of the first activities Marty does when he starts a new role is ask a lot of questions. Marty shared that he "spends the better part of three months talking to people at all levels and asking them what is working, what is not working, why it works, why it doesn't work." From there, Marty goes beyond those traditional questions and puts his new colleagues into the driver's seat of change by asking, "If you could change things and you were the CEO, what would you do?" While Marty sources great advice, he also establishes fantastic rapport that lasts beyond onboarding. "If you really want to know what is going on, talk to the people in the organization. If you focus on getting input from just one perspective, like the C-suite or frontline managers, you will miss out on a lot of valuable information. By getting a broader perspective, you gain an understanding of where everybody is and what the organization's short- and long-term objectives are to align your strategic HR business plan with the initiatives of the company."

Figure 4–1. *HR Like a Boss* rockstar Marty Guastella

It's a "People Business"

Once you have clarity and alignment with the vision and purpose, set out to get to know the people. The easiest way to do this is to go to the places where your business does its business (and I do not mean all of your restrooms). Like Cindy, regularly visit various sites like regional hubs, retail locations, warehouses, distribution centers, or sales offices. As a result, you will inherently meet the people of your organization. This is where you can find the organization's intellectual gold that can further drive positive change, align a more meaningful purpose, and deliver improved results. The countless examples found by the Undercover Bosses led to impactful changes for the corporate office, and more importantly, for the people the boss met. Employees are the lifeblood of your company and want to be heard. All too often, executives, leaders, and HR pros avoid or do not ask employees for their opinions. Employees have the perfect vantage point on what is going on and understand what it takes to improve business operations. They are full of amazing ideas and insights on making those meaningful changes. All you have to do is ask.

Additional Resources . . . Right Under Your Nose

Another important but often overlooked site to visit is your company's website. It is amazing how much information is available for the public, yet internal employees rarely spend substantial time studying the content. In this vein, your company's website should include things like purpose and core values, products and services, leadership team bios, locations, and so on. But dig into your company's products and services—all of them—and how they are positioned and differentiated from the competition. What is your website telling the outside world that makes your organization special? After doing a thorough review of the site, meet with your marketing team to get to know them, ask specific questions about the website and marketing materials, and share some of the feedback that you may have. They would love to hear from you. Marketing teams are dying for employees to share their feedback and tell the story of the company.

The final step in getting to know your company may feel a bit like your Accounting 101 class in your sophomore year of college. However, it is a critical step in studying your company. First, review the details of any public or company-provided financials. The profit and loss (P&L) is typically the best at telling your company's story. In it, you should find details about your revenue sources, cost of goods sold (COGS), indirect expenses, and profitability. Most companies shoot for their COGS to be 20–60 percent of their sales, and their profit to be 15 percent of their revenue. The lower the COGS percentage, the better. The higher the profit-to-revenue percentage, the better. These numbers provide details about the health of your organization. Another common financial report is the balance sheet. This report shows your company's assets that are balanced by your liabilities and equity.

Once you have studied the company's financials, schedule a meeting with a member of your accounting or finance team to dig further into the numbers. In a small water vending business we own together, my partner, Todd Baughman, taught me many years ago that "the numbers never lie." He is right. When going through the

Profit & Loss	YTD	% of Rev.
Revenue	$ 6,254,982.13	100.00%
Cost of Goods Sold	$ (3,245,892.22)	-51.89%
Gross Profit	$ 3,009,089.91	48.11%
Expenses	$ (2,004,000.25)	-32.04%
Net Operating Income	$ 1,005,089.66	16.07%
Other Income	$ 2,424.99	0.04%
Other Expenses	$ (1,004.19)	-0.02%
Net Income	$ 1,006,510.46	16.09%

Figure 4–2. Example of a monthly profit and loss statement

details of your organization's P&L or balance sheet, be prepared with questions about the ratios of one category to another like revenue to COGS or revenue to profit. Seek to understand the meaning of the numbers and any good or bad trends that exist. This will help you better understand and influence your company's most impactful profit components.

Yes, this can get very technical. Some of you might be saying, "I got into HR because I hate numbers or failed at math or accounting." Sorry, people who do *HR Like a Boss* do not make that excuse. Remember, the numbers tell an important story.

Your ~~Question~~ Answer Checklist

At the end of the day, the exercise of getting to know your company aligns with the value or lack thereof that HR is bringing to the business. If you do not take the time to initially discover the what, who, how, and why of your organization, you will be starting at a disadvantage. So, seek answers to questions that HR doesn't always seek, yet are critical to know, including the following:

» How does the business work?
» How do we make money and lose money?
» How do the pieces (departments, products, service offerings, etc.) fit together? If there are three divisions, take the time to understand each and what makes them profitable (or not).
» How can I help the business do more of what makes it successful and less of what makes it unsuccessful?
» What's the value your business is delivering to customers?
» What are the business's goals?
» What will make the business reach its goal, and how can I help?
» What is the health of the business? Is it growing? Or has it matured?

Your study, along with the conversations with peers across departments, blue- and white-collar employees, and your bosses will provide an understanding of your company, its industry, and the niche your organization is filling. With this information, you are setting the foundation to think differently about influencing and improving your organization and its people.

Be Emotionally Aware

How are you feeling?

Later on in this chapter, I share why those four words could be the most important learning opportunity you glean from this book. I cannot and will not take credit for it, but I will share its importance in your ability to think differently.

As we put a bow on thinking differently, we dissect the constantly evolving and complex concept of emotional intelligence. It feels like this topic has become somewhat synonymous with the human resources function. Why is it so difficult for people to wrap their arms around this thing so eloquently (or maybe not) called EQ?

I'm about to share my personal emotional intelligence journey and highlight some of the great business leaders and resources that have helped me in the ever-evolving aspect of EQ. In doing so, I hope you pull some meaningful nuggets out and learn some emotional tools to do some amazingly awesome HR.

Before digging into my voyage, please allow me to share this fundamental note: learning, developing, and evolving your emotional intelligence is a highly personal endeavor. With that said, my experience tells me that it is much more difficult to embark on this trek by yourself. Over the next few pages, I share my personal experiences that have allowed me to evolve and grow continuously when developing my emotional intelligence.

JB's Emotional Intelligence Journey

Having committed my professional life to serving the HR professional, EQ comes up again and again. I can't remember the first time the concept of emotional intelligence was shared with me. Not remembering that moment, I am sure I blew it off and continued on with my day, not realizing how profoundly impactful the concept of emotional intelligence would be on my personal and professional life. As the author of this book, I guess I could make up a story about the overpowering moment that I realized the importance of emotional intelligence. There is no such story, but instead several small, unmemorable experiences that led to my moment.

Here I go again with an eighties reference. Ironically, that moment was kind of like watching the eighties' synth-pop band a-ha's, "Take on Me" video on MTV for the very first time (when MTV used to play actual *music* videos). Do you remember how cool it was when the videographer merged the pencil-sketched story with the band's live rendition? I was mesmerized. Thank goodness for YouTube for those of you who weren't fortunate enough to live through this iconic MTV moment.

Emotional intelligence is all about taking on yourself to realize the emotions you are feeling and then sensibly and knowingly using your emotions to your advantage. You are literally taking on yourself in a way that you never knew possible—it is a mind-blowing experience. Don't you think it is ironic that the title of that a-ha song, "Take on Me," aligns so well to my emotional intelligence a-ha! moment?

What got me to finally realize that EQ was a cornerstone for personal and professional success was seeing its impact on others and their passion for the importance of understanding, studying, and constantly working on their emotional intelligence. I saw how people who harnessed their emotions impacted the lives of many close friends, colleagues, and family, in both positive and negative ways. In addition, my professional coach and therapist, Dr. Melissa Briggs-Phillips, has forced me most kindly and encouragingly to lean into my emotions and carefully acknowledge my feelings to sensibly use my emotions in a way that is best for those around me.

As a result of Dr. Melissa's tutelage and guidance, I saw the positive impact strong EQ had on personal and professional lives. I committed to growing my knowledge and improving my awareness and management of my own emotions in order to advance my professional relationships. As a result, the work I put in expanded into my personal life, causing me to strive to have the skills and abilities to be a better husband, son, father, brother, and friend.

The first step in my EQ journey started with very strong reflection and, in some sense, dealing with how I was raised relative to my emotional awareness. I grew up in a loving home with wonderful parents. They loved me dearly and paved the path for me to achieve whatever I desired in my life. On top of that, my siblings were and are amazing people. Growing up, we rarely fought, and we simply had a ton of fun. Our childhood was blessed with many wonderful experiences, and I do not recall a tremendous number of hardships that would expose many good and bad things in a family unit.

Upon reflection, one thing did become clear to me: we did not talk about or express our feelings and emotions. My parents did many things right and were a tremendous example in countless ways, but they did not exemplify acknowledging and expressing emotions. I justify this missed opportunity by telling myself it was how they were raised.

I first met Dr. Melissa Briggs-Phillips at the Human Resources Association of Central Ohio (HRACO, the Columbus-area SHRM chapter) in 2018, and her unique perspective has had a lasting impact on my approach to feelings, relationships, and business. There were roughly three hundred HR pros in the room listening to her presentation on emotional well-being in the workplace, but I felt that Dr. Melissa was talking to me and only me. Her message resonated as she discussed the struggles of executives, especially men, to connect with their own emotions, let alone those of other people.

Dr. Melissa's direct and occasionally (appropriate) expletive communication style was and is exactly what I needed to navigate through a challenging time in my life. She suggests that "emotions are like energy—not created or destroyed—they just change shape. While family systems may not admit emotions are happening, they are and do not go away." She goes on to say, "Feelings are like an energy circuit that needs to be completed. Emotions that are willfully ignored are just repackaged. If sadness is deemed unacceptable, it can become displayed as anger, an eating disorder, an unhealthy relationship with alcohol—just to name a handful of possible outcomes."

Early on in my life, I aspired to become a professional golfer. I was conditioned to "control" my emotions as it was beneficial to me on the golf course, which was my primary athletic focus as a kid. If you ever watch a professional golf tournament, you will not see a lot of emotional ups and downs from the players on tour. I modeled the behavior I saw on TV and even worked with a sports psychologist to hone this skill. If a PGA or LPGA golfer was overly expressive with positive and negative emotions, they were considered brash and out of control. For some time, this worked to my advantage as I maintained my emotions whether I made a terrible shot or an unbelievable putt. Many of the golfers whom I played with struggled to maintain their composure, resulting in a roller-coaster ride of emotions as their scorecards included a myriad of scores. As a result, I earned a scholarship to play Division I golf at Kent State University.

However, my aspirations to be a professional golfer waned as the reality of the minuscule chances that I had to play on the PGA Tour sunk in. After falling in love with who turned out to be my wife, my purpose shifted to starting a family and supporting it by starting my own businesses.

As I continued to push forward to achieve the results in my life that I desired, I ran into one major obstacle. In my 20s the fact that

I did not have a good pulse on my feelings and emotions caused me tremendous strife as I found myself depressed and overwhelmed with life. Part of this evolution came from seeing my wife and her family express a wide array of emotions and feelings. Even more shocking and disturbing to me was the fact that they talked about them openly and without reservation. I recall many dinner conversations at the Dodds' house that included topics like how you feel when your hormones kick in during your period, the embarrassment of a zit on your face, the emotion of a new crush one of the kids had on a classmate, the heartbreak of a relationship gone bad, or the intense frustration one of the parents had with their siblings. When I first observed these expressions of emotions, it felt like a whole new world, one that I had not lived during my first twenty years. Nothing was taboo in this family, and they talked about everything and anything. On top of that, they were full of life and expressed a wide range of emotions. It was a life that I was not familiar with in many respects.

At some point, I tried to join in the exuberant fun and awkwardly shared how I was feeling. It was incredibly difficult for me, so I regressed to my reticent and unemotional way. Eventually, I became incredibly defensive and not open to feedback from my wife or coaching at work. I found I was especially defensive regarding feedback from domineering people—those whom I would later label as micromanagers.

Thanks to the encouragement of my wife, I began to seek professional counseling and went to meet Dr. Sharon Irwin. I began to uncomfortably talk about my feelings and the things that affected my life. It was an eye-opening experience, and one that I will never forget. I remember the first time I walked into Dr. Irwin's office and wondered how many people were staring at me knowing that I had something wrong with me. I felt a tremendous amount of shame and considered driving away.

My time with Dr. Irwin helped me identify what was going on and why it was happening. Luckily, I found that talking about my feelings and understanding my emotions became a revelatory experience. It was like a whole new world, a world in which it was okay to have ups and downs and highs and lows. Had I turned around at that first appointment, I would never have experienced being okay with my emotions.

Another milestone in my EQ journey came nearly twenty years later as my company embarked on a firmwide, multiyear training and workshopping adventure as we read and debated three best-selling books: *Emotional Intelligence 2.0* by Jean Greaves and Travis Bradberry; *Crucial Conversations* by Kerry Patterson, Joseph Grenny, Ron McMillan, and Al Switzler; and *Crucial Accountability* by Kerry Patterson, Joseph Grenny, Ron McMillan, Al Switzler, and David Maxfield.

Our firm went through an intense book club that included dissecting every single chapter and having open team discussions about personal and professional applications of how emotions impact the way to do business in our professional and personal lives. It was important to me that our team create an open, honest, and direct work environment where team members could work through challenges, issues, and opportunities without the involvement of a manager or professional moderator. Learning these concepts and eventually living by them set the foundation for Willory to embrace our purpose of "We Empower People" and set up our team to successfully live by our core values on a consistent basis.

The next monumental step in my EQ journey occurred shortly after my dad passed. He eventually lost his life at 81-years-old after a six-month battle with pancreatic cancer. During his last three months, my dad moved in with my family, and I had the honor of taking care of him. Those ninety days changed me forever, having endured my dad falling while taking a shower resulting in ten stitches to his head, the arrival of COVID-19 onto US soil, in-home palliative care, and his eventual passing in a hospice care facility that had four different visitation policies in the eight days he was there (thanks to the ever-changing regulations and understanding of COVID-19).

The day after my dad passed away was a brutal twenty-four hours. Afterward, I struggled to get motivated to work and isolated myself from my family despite being in lockdown and limiting my outside interaction with the world to runs to the post office and to get gasoline in my car. When I finally came down from the emotions of it all and the grief of losing my two biggest fans in less than thirteen months set in, the absence of their unconditional love became very real.

Eventually, I went numb to it all and droned along trying to get through the day just to have those eight hours when numbness went away while I slept.

At the peak of my heartbreak, I had scheduled a therapy appointment with Dr. Melissa Briggs-Phillips, who was struggling with her own proverbial shit show caring for her clients in an apex of concern, despair, hopelessness, and anxiety. I still remember the five minutes before my scheduled virtual visit when I prayed Dr. Melissa would not call me. I had sunk to a place where I simply did not want to deal with all I had been through and the emotional vacuum that existed.

Luckily for me, Dr. Melissa did call, and we navigated together through the unique place where I found myself. She encouraged me to get grief counseling, which I had already scheduled. Then, we dove into the fact that I felt desensitized and had a sense of dullness that I had never experienced before. At that moment, it became clear to her what was going on. For the next two weeks, she recommended that I record at least six times the exact feeling or emotion that I was experiencing during the day. She was certain that it might be harder than I thought and to not kid myself by trying to only record positive emotions. Dr. Melissa informed me of the phenomenon of toxic positivity that can exist when trying to persevere through trying and difficult times. She suggested that "the emotional severity of the global pandemic highlighted something for the broader culture that therapists have known for a long time . . . that it is okay to *not* be okay."

During the onset of the global pandemic, there was a significant increase in memes and social media posts with the phrase "toxic positivity," and it struck me that it was about time for people to hear this message! Individuals and companies usually do not have nefarious intent when they default to suggestions like staying positive, looking on the bright side, and knowing it will all work out! However, doing so creates avoidance of the full story and denial of someone's lived experience of pain and hurt. Toxic positivity skips the necessary steps of honoring what you are feeling to move forward effectively.

On top of all of that, Dr. Melissa recommended that I listen to a couple of podcasts, including Brené Brown's interview with Dr. Marc Brackett. It turned out to be a life-changing recommendation for me. More to come shortly on that.

At the end of that call with Dr. Melissa, I felt like I had hope. There was a plan and a list of tasks for me to complete to try to work through what was going on. Over the next two weeks, I religiously recorded how I felt, ranging from depressed, despair, hopeful, joyful, sad, lonely, and about thirty other uniquely distinct feelings. As Dr. Melissa had predicted, it was a tough exercise for me to find the precise label for the emotion that I was feeling. A few days in, I felt like a little kid who discovered an unknown treasure in his backyard. I was exhilarated to recognize that I was having all these emotions when in my mind I felt numb and that someone had given me the permission to feel.

During that fateful two weeks of emotional growth, I listened to Brené Brown's podcast interview with Dr. Marc Brackett.[2] The childish fandom that Brené had fawning over Marc's work grabbed my immediate attention. Brené used words like practical, actionable, and tactical to describe his book *Permission to Feel: Unlocking the Power of Emotions to Help Our Kids, Ourselves, and Our Society Thrive.*[3]

2. "Dr. Marc Brackett and Brené on 'Permission to Feel,'" interview by Brené Brown, *Unlocking Us*, April 2020, https://brenebrown.com/podcast/dr-marc-brackett-and-brene-on-permission-to-feel/.

3. Marc Brackett, *Permission to Feel: Unlock the Power of Emotions to Help Our Kids, Ourselves, and Our Society Thrive* (London: Quercus Publishing, 2019).

Like Brené, I was in awe of Marc's work. First, I was impressed by his eminent passion and knowledge on the topic of emotional intelligence. The passion for EQ oozed out of him, and the incredible number of tools and resources he had developed in order to achieve his life's passion were inspiring.

The resources that Marc offered were things like the Mood Meter, an app that allows you to recognize and label the emotions you are feeling at any time, in any place, twenty-four seven. Marc has also made himself available through a free book club, during which he walks readers through each chapter, giving them unfettered access (thanks to Zoom) to how he views the world of EQ. In addition, he cofounded the Oji Life Lab, where they developed the Emotion Life Lab, a digital learning system for businesses that helps people develop essential emotional intelligence skills that drive performance at work and in life.

I really began to dig into what I was hearing, reading, and feeling. The only way to help others harness the power of strong emotional intelligence is by authentically living that way ourselves in our personal and professional lives. It feels like that moment when a flight attendant prepares for liftoff on a commercial flight and encourages passengers to affix their own oxygen mask before helping anyone else if the cabin becomes depressurized.

In Marc's book and throughout his work, he frames the definition of EQ in a profound and simple way. In essence, to Marc EQ is using your emotions *wisely* versus trying to control them. To me, the key word in his definition is wisely (hence the italics).

Despite years of trying, I have found it is impossible to make my negative and depressing feelings and emotions simply go away. If I am uncomfortable with whatever I am feeling, I have found through life experience that I cannot suppress those feelings by encapsulating my uncomfortable emotions in a glass jar with a seal-tight lid. Marc shared that the mindset of trying to control our emotions is an issue. By taking his wisdom and making it my own, I have reframed how I define EQ.

Speaking of wise, Marc encourages everyone to become an emotion scientist. This was a concept that took me a bit to wrap my head around, but the more I thought about it, the concept became crystal clear (said in my best impression of the Jack Nicholson voice). When I hear the word "scientist," I think of someone who is smart and challenges the status quo. They use data to prove or disprove ideas and tinker with details countless times before getting it right. Scientists experiment with a lot of theories and drive innovations that lead to new inventions that change the world for the better. The use of the phrase "emotion scientist" finally sunk in with me when I affiliated the term "explorer" with the idea of a scientist. To me, a scientist is insatiably curious and can get fixated on something. As a result, they dig into topics with intense interest to better understand what is going on. Scientists normally do not come to an immediate conclusion when faced with a challenge or problem. Instead, they take a step back, observe what is happening, study what is going on, and begin to play out scenarios in their head or in a lab.

Having a fix-the-problem-at-hand mentality, my immediate and instinctive reaction to most issues is to solve the challenge in front of me and move on to the next one. As I have gained more experience and knowledge, I have found that approach to be fraught with issues, many of them having to do with the emotions created by the situation instead of the actual, tangible issue. As a result, I have worked hard to become incredibly curious about my own emotions and feelings while encouraging others to do the same.

As you can tell, I have been highly influenced by Marc Brackett's work.

Why does EQ matter? I hope you have a personal answer to that question that inspires you to continue learning and developing your emotional intelligence. You will encounter many circumstances in the workplace that range from unemotional to highly emotional. These emotions are cues, and the instinct is to approach or avoid.

The importance of employees' emotional and physical health has never been more important. Recent studies have shown there is a direct correlation between a leader's emotional intelligence and its effect on employees' physical and mental health. I encourage HR professionals to learn how to take care of themselves first so that they can bring their best selves to serving the needs of others. In my journey to improve my mental well-being, I constantly give myself that permission to feel, aspire to be curious and interested in others' feelings, and use my emotions as wisely as possible.

We devoted this entire section to thinking differently. You must exercise and relax your brain to grow and develop. Learning, exploring, thinking, strategizing, and reflecting are all exercises that someone doing *HR Like a Boss* makes time for consistently.

Once we are at a good place in our own minds, we can set the example to help those in our organization, network, and family become great professionals and, more importantly, even better human beings.

Embracing what makes you and others unique and feeling empowered to think differently puts you in an ideal place to celebrate human resources' different thoughts, emotions, perspectives, ideas, and more—setting you up to do *HR Like a Boss*.

Now that you have given thinking differently a chance, let's dive into how the HR profession can begin to be different and, more importantly, be better.

After all of that, I cannot resist asking the question that I started this chapter with: How are you feeling?

Part III
Be Different

Chapter 5
The Boss Mindset

Once you've adjusted your thinking to a boss mindset, it's time to put thoughts into action and actually *be* different by doing HR differently and, more specifically, better. My dad used to call it "putting your money where your mouth is" or "practicing what you preach." So, let's do *HR Like a Boss* and actually be different!

Overcoming Baggage

Unfortunately, even as you change your behaviors, you still have to overcome the frustration directed toward HR that can come from executives, employees, and stakeholders. It may not be accurate, but perception often reflects reality, and many executives and business leaders perceive human resources overhead to be best suited to writing handbooks, party planning, and firing employees. So, when you start being different, you will need to overcome the box you're currently in—and that box is often not one with an "executive leadership" label on it. Being different, leading, overcoming past perceptions (and maybe realities), and striving to do *HR Like a Boss* means earning the right to be taken more seriously.

Something about this book caught your attention. Maybe it was the catchy name or the strange spelling of the author's last name.

You are reading this book for a reason, and I will assume that reason is in the spirit of getting better at what you do. To transform the perceptions about the HR function, each HR professional must take well-thought-out action. This chapter highlights several steps that professionals who do *HR Like a Boss* typically take.

Being different starts with a willingness to be flexible and adaptable as a business. The world changes—sometimes slowly, sometimes on a dime—but doing *HR Like a Boss* means you can change with it. Being different means striving to be better every day and constantly adapting to today's business realities from both a macro (the world and industry at large) and micro (a challenge specific to your business) perspective. Markets change, business climates change, and personal circumstances change. If you do not anticipate these changes, you and your business could get passed by. Adapting *HR Like a Boss* means recognizing modifications are coming!

Pandemic Realities

All of us are (way too) familiar with the pandemic and the paradigm shift it brought to our work lives. Work-from-home went from a nice-to-have to an absolute necessity to minimize our person-to-person interactions and maintain safe social distancing at work. Businesses quickly adjusted, and as a result, there were rampant layoffs, industries decimated, leaders exposed, protective measures taken to survive, and legislation passed to provide business funding and regulate safe work environments.

And, as I am sure you are aware, HR was at the forefront of it all. The enormous disruption of the pandemic forced HR to take a front-row seat and manage the (primarily negative) impacts on businesses and their employees. Did you embrace these challenges and take the mantle of leadership, or did you mostly follow and take the lead from someone else? To do *HR Like a Boss*, we must actively lead our organization and positively impact our employees, organization, and community.

As a staffing and consulting firm serving the HR community, our business experienced negative impacts from the global pandemic. We felt the tremendous stress and weight of the unique circumstances as our clients wrestled with cutbacks rather than expansion and investments. On the positive side, since our firm was founded as a 100 percent virtual business, we were positioned to serve our clients while being incredibly careful and mindful of our team members' best interests. While I hope that this is one of the most disruptive changes that the world and business community will face, we must remain vigilant and stand ready to deal with whatever comes our way—good or bad.

We saw the worst of people during the pandemic as many were afraid and resistant to the necessary changes to stay safe, protect lives, and stay in business. Why are we so fearful of change? We know that people are creatures of habit and tend to gravitate to a comfortable place of repetition, doing things the same way over and over again. In normal times, we do not take the time to ask if our habits are flawed or overly time-consuming. Routines and comfort are the enemies of change. We naturally avoid change instead of running toward disruption. Fear of the unknown fills in the blanks with stories to justify inaction to try to improve or change.

Yes, You Can

This negative (and wrong) "I can't change" narrative, combined with the amount of work required to change, paralyzes people into a state of internally justifying the status quo. As a discipline that often promotes standards and compliance, it's natural for HR to embrace the status quo. It is easy to get comfortable with what has "always" worked. Challenging *HR Like a Boss* means you are not okay with the status quo. The business world is constantly changing. As an HR professional doing *HR Like a Boss*, fight the fear of the unknown and embrace change.

You must lead through change and promote the naturally occurring business disruptions as good things! We saw the HR community embrace this mindset during Jennifer McClure's DisruptHR movement, a worldwide phenomenon in which HR and business professionals get together to network and learn from speakers who are required to make their disruptive points impacting HR in five minutes or less. The HR community flocked to this concept.

McClure, while reflecting on the success of DisruptHR, said, "Our vision was to get HR professionals together in a fun, innovative format where people could share ideas. We honestly never thought of it as a business . . . maybe we should have! It's built a great community of more than five thousand people sharing their stories globally."

Clearly, a segment of the HR community loves some disruption. Just because a lot of people are resistant to change doesn't mean all of us are! Avoid complacency or the idea of feeling smug or content with your accomplishments. I don't know about you, but I never like to see the word "smug" in the list of words to describe me.

If you're looking to make a difference in people's lives, truly impact the organization that you work for, and leave a positive imprint on your community, you need to fight complacency, run toward change, inspire disruptions, aspire to transform, and be different (in a better way) in how you approach your craft.

HR Fundamentals Are Assumed

As a foundational piece of doing *HR Like a Boss*, it is assumed that you know what you are doing and have the skills, knowledge, and experience to do it well. This reminds me of my Aunt Irene, who would always joke by teaching me and anyone else who was paying attention that "if you assume, you make an *ass* out of *you* and *me*."

Let's buck this cliché and not make anyone look like an ass. If you are in the human resources profession reading this book, I am going to assume that you know what you are doing. I have faith that you won't prove me wrong.

Let's draw a parallel using our rock 'n' roll boss, Bruce Springsteen. Sustaining his boss moniker by filling stadiums with adoring fans, innovating new platforms, selling out Broadway, and continuing to produce hit albums, Bruce must have the fundamentals of singing and playing music down pat. Now, as we know, Bruce does WAY more than that. He doesn't just put out albums with cover songs on them . . . he writes and composes music with soulful, personal, and meaningful lyrics. And he can't just go on the road and simply sing for two hours, say "hello" and "goodnight" . . . he needs to captivate the crowd with his charisma and storytelling to be The Boss! It's his ability to go above and beyond the typical concert with stories, iconic songs, and long setlists that makes Bruce *the* original boss.

In this section, we focus on the first step. Let's call this step the fundamentals of performing. Like me, I am sure you have heard many examples of what happens to a house when it has foundation issues.

When I think about fundamentals, I think of the legendarily neurotic and obsessed professional athlete Kobe Bryant. Like a great golfer perfecting the basics of grip pressure on a golf club, Kobe Bryant's insane infatuation with the most basic basketball fundamentals, like footwork, was chronicled in a YouTube video published by Alan Stein Jr. two months after the preeminent athlete's death. According to Stein, Kobe would put in an unparalleled level of effort and unmatched focus on the most basic items and tactics.[1] Kobe first focused on the basics before putting any work into the more intricate and difficult basketball moves like a fadeaway jumper or baby hook shot. When Stein asked Kobe why he was still putting

---

1. Alan Stein Jr., "Kobe Bryant's Insane Obsession with the Basics," YouTube, March 25, 2020, https://www.youtube.com/watch?v=RYtUq8a5Er8.

so much work into such basic drills, the "Black Mamba" politely responded, "Why do you think I am the best player in the world? Because I never get bored with the basics."

Stein suggested in his piece that Kobe "taught me a life-changing lesson. Just because something is basic, it does not mean it is easy. If it was easy, everyone else would be doing it." While our society may tell us it is okay to skip steps and bypass the process, the real sacrifice is mastering the basics. The key to improving performance in anything we do is to identify the basics or fundamentals and be relentlessly committed to performing them with consistency. That is hard. Basics can be boring, mundane, and monotonous. However, often the basics are what separates the average from the good, the good from the great, and the great from the GOAT (greatest of all time). Stein ended his piece by stating that "the highest performers have found a way to fall in love (there is that word again) with the basics and make them a part of their daily routine."

In the case of an HR professional, becoming the GOAT starts with a solid understanding of the macro aspects of human resources—the kind of stuff they teach in an HR 101 class. Having a deep understanding of the common principles of HR—including employee relations, recruitment and selection, performance man-agement, learning and development, succession planning, compen-sation, benefits, payroll, HR technology, and analytics—puts you in a position to deliver for your people and the organization. For those who practice in a more general capacity, your HR duties are broad. Learning about and asking the experts in each of these areas will help you master the basics of HR. For others, your primary responsibility may cause you to focus on a particular discipline like compensation, HR technology, or payroll. It is up to you to get the basics down before exploring the next-level areas.

As previously mentioned, someone doing *HR Like a Boss* does not stop there. We cannot get to the next level without mastering the current level. This is why video games are so popular. As some-one goes from level to level, they achieve more in the game. People who are great and stand out from the crowd thrive on leveling up. You should too!

That leveling up could start with learning new technical skills and becoming an expert in your field. Once you have the basics down, set yourself apart through your ability to master your interpersonal skills and always be improving your decision-making, conflict management, effective communication, technology usage, and positive influence over others (the list goes on and on).

Ever heard of the saying, "There is no shame in a shameless plug?" I assume not, as I just made it up to justify this not-so-subtle hint. If you are confident in your fundamentals and looking for a way to go to the next level, join the *HR Like a Boss* training series and community at www.hrlikeaboss.com. As a part of the training, you can gain access to the *HR Like a Boss* training community which was designed to help HR professionals grow and develop their HR and business skills. In the training, I start with the basics of doing *HR Like a Boss* by dissecting the five main principles of this book. On top of that, the training provides real-life examples and tips not found in this book to help you become an amazingly awesome HR pro. To top it off, we have created a community as an avenue to connect with other amazingly awesome HR pros to create fellowship, share your experiences, and learn from each other along with unique and meaningful content that you cannot find anywhere else.

Grow Your Knowledge or Get Out of HR

I've detailed the importance of mastering the fundamentals of HR before progressing to next-level concepts and practices. The following list showcases the basics to next-level learning and development opportunities to increase your knowledge base. Someone who does *HR Like a Boss* checks off most of these boxes. However, they realize that learning is a lifelong, iterative journey that never ends.

Over the next few pages, I dive into this "Grow Your HR Knowledge" checklist:

» Earn basic education (online HR courses or, better yet, HR degree).

» Complete Society for Human Resources Management (SHRM)-related courses and learning events.

» Network with other HR professionals.

» Consume HR and business blogs, books, and podcasts.

» Gain HR certifications (SHRM-SCP or SHRM-CP).

» Establish mentor/mentee relationship(s).

» Site visit of the HR team at another company that you look to emulate.

» Earn business education (MBA, Executive MBA, etc.).

» Shadow or ride along with other departments in your business.

» Learn the business through a stint in operations, sales, marketing, accounting, or IT.

» Expose yourself to different cultures through an international assignment, volunteer opportunity, or serve on a nonprofit board.

» Join the *HR Like a Boss* community (okay, this is a very shameless plug) and gain access to an impactful training course, informative content, and community of amazingly awesome HR colleagues.

I hope as you read through the list that you said to yourself, "I have done most of that." Awesome. You are on your way. Now, for those who are not that boastful, that's fine too. There is a lot on this list that takes decades to complete. And again, learning is iterative and should be a lifelong aspiration.

First on the list is basic education. Countless programs throughout the United States and the world offer advanced education in human resources. Regarding basic education, you can also find an abundance of online and traditional courses available to take that first step toward building your HR foundation.

Now, let's look at the opportunities offered through SHRM. It is almost staggering to consider the number of opportunities to learn through SHRM. As the leading organization for people and workplaces, SHRM provides abundant resources to those who work in HR at organizations. SHRM offers national and local membership opportunities, learning tools to advance the profession, endless resources to support the HR professional, trade publications for thought leaders and influencers to share their experiences, and countless online and in-person events. My earnest recommendation is based upon twenty years of firsthand experience seeing the impact of endless opportunities for fellowship and learning afforded by being a part of SHRM. Becoming a member and getting involved in SHRM at a national or local level is an excellent step in growing your knowledge in HR.

In addition to utilizing the great resources provided by SHRM, let me suggest two other easy ways to develop your network of smart, experienced, and seasoned HR professionals who, collectively, are at different points in their careers. Start by asking your existing network, "Who is the best HR professional you know?" Once you get a response, simply ask to be introduced to that HR professional.

After you have made initial contact, it will take a few interactions between you and the HR professional to see if you and this person are a good fit for one another. This process is kind of like dating. It will happen naturally—you will connect with some of the people with whom you network, and there will be others with whom you will not. I would strongly suggest being cordial to all and spending time fostering relationships with those with whom you develop a meaningful connection. This means reaching out to them regularly, taking an interest in them personally, getting to know their family and other friends, and making an effort to remember important dates like anniversaries and birthdays. Often, LinkedIn will remind you of these, so it is less remembering than monitoring these reminders.

Next, great thought leaders, influencers, authors, and general practitioners are putting out insightful HR and business content in book, blog, and podcast form. Remember, doing *HR Like a Boss* is not only about HR but about making a positive impact on your business and the community. Expanding your knowledge base beyond human resources and into business and community content could be incredibly impactful. Find the best authors who speak to you and consume their content through the means that best fit your lifestyle. Knowing they are just people and not intimidating figures, look to connect with them through social media. When reaching out to them, share why you are connecting and what their work has meant to you.

Get That Piece of Paper

If you want to distinguish yourself as an HR professional, get a certification. Once you make time in your schedule to earn an advanced HR certification like SHRM-CP, SHRM-SCP, PHR, SPHR, aPHR (associates), and GPHR (global), you will set yourself apart. Additionally, you can get a more specialized certification in CCP (compensation), CBP (benefits), HRIP (technology), CPP (payroll), FPC (payroll), and PMP (projects).

Because of the educational, social, and financial impact of getting your SHRM certification, I have decided to donate a portion of the proceeds from the sale of this book and any other revenue generated from the *HR Like a Boss* assets to pay for the testing cost of the SHRM certification for graduating seniors on the verge of getting their college degree in human resources. Having a purpose in what you do is paramount to doing *HR Like a Boss*, and we felt it was important to walk the walk, not just talk the talk.

Some would argue that the most insightful education you can get is by observing others perform the job or duties, allowing you to emulate their moves and learn from their experiences and mistakes. This reminds me of why Phil Mickelson, Hall of Fame golfer and Tiger Woods's closest rival, is a left-handed golfer. When he was a young kid, he would watch his dad swing a golf club. Then, he began to copy his swing by standing across from his dad and mirroring his dad's backswing and following through the swing. The only way he could do that was to get on the other side of the ball and follow his dad's right-handed golf swing. This turned out to be a fantastic way to mirror his dad's golf swing. For golf fans, the rest is history and it's a fun surprise to learn that "Lefty" is right-handed!

In this spirit, establishing a small and very intimate set of mentors is critical for accelerating your success in business and HR. The sooner you find others with track records and more experience in succeeding and failing, the quicker you will learn invaluable lessons. This shortens your learning curve while simultaneously developing life-changing relationships. We should *always* have mentors, no matter how experienced or seasoned we feel we are. At the right time, give back to your community by providing mentorship to an aspiring mentee. Take tremendous pride and effort in that responsibility as you shape your mentees' future.

Let's do some legal cheating in the spirit of learning from others. You must have heard through the grapevine about or marveled at the success of another organization in your community. This particular company appears to be doing everything right, gets recognized in the community for its efforts, and has a leg up in attracting and retaining talent. Through the network you have established, find a colleague who works at a company you admire or someone you know connected with this pinnacle of employers. When you initiate contact, be open and honest with why you are reaching out. You might meet resistance or flattery. If your connection does not agree or seems standoffish, it is okay. Go find someone else or another organization doing things the right way. Once you find someone willing to participate and help, look to schedule a time to grab lunch, coffee, or a beer (either in person or via Zoom) and begin to ask a bunch of questions. Ultimately, a site visit would be ideal, during which you can dive into specifics and details about their purpose, people, productivity, processes, and profit. My guess is you'll find some helpful nuggets and realize that the euphoric perception you created is probably not 100 percent true, as every organization has warts and blemishes. What is most fascinating is how they attack these issues or shortcomings to minimize their negative effect on the company, people, and culture.

We are going to the next level by exploring an MBA or master's in HR. This is rarefied air with less than 10 percent of business professionals carrying an advanced degree. As told in my earlier story, my college education ended with a bachelor's degree. I do recall my dad's investment of time (weekends for two years straight) to get his executive MBA from Baldwin Wallace University. To improve his business skills, he made the sacrifice of spending this precious time attending class and studying as opposed to spending time with his family during his weekends off work. Getting an MBA is a significant commitment. For those that have done it, there are few regrets *after* it is done.

My friend and boss-like HR pro Lauren Rudman was fortunate enough to go straight from undergrad to an MBA.

"I went to Cleveland State University for my MBA, and the program helped because it included general business courses," explained Rudman. "Constantly hearing about business and being taught to understand business in my MBA program combined with mentors as well as professional organizations helped prepare me to be a business-centric HR professional."

But Don't Forget the Practical

Just as imperative (or more, really) than an advanced degree is real-life experience. As we chronicled with Cindy Torres Essell, tremendous HR knowledge can be garnered from spending time in the field with team members and associates of your business. Take the time to do a ride-along with your sales team, schedule a day-in-the-life of your accounting manager, or shadow (or pitch in for) your customer service team. You will learn about the practicalities, or lack thereof, of HR policies and procedures. Not to mention, you will earn some street cred with your employees as you will show a genuine interest in what they are doing and how they are doing it.

Finally, my apologies for another shameless plug. I could not write this book without providing an additional resource to help you make an impact in an amazingly awesome way so you can do *HR Like a Boss*. Consider being a part of a community that practices *HR Like a Boss*. We have developed a social learning platform providing next-level tutelage and networking on all of the subjects covered in this book, including but not limited to ownership, love, thinking differently, being different, being better, taking action, and making an impact. It is a unique mix of HR fundamentals, personal reflection, peer networking, and advanced interpersonal skills development. The learning tools and community will help you develop your HR and business skills and knowledge based upon the principles of this book. Check it out at www.hrlikeaboss.com.

I put a warning at the beginning regarding the importance of changing the perception of HR for a reason. If you are not willing to make the sacrifices needed to advance your career and become the best possible HR professional that *you* can, I *strongly* recommend that you do some personal soul-searching. You need to do your personal best, but not at the expense of your well-being, relationships, or sense of self. If you cannot make this commitment, develop a plan to get out of HR. How could I be so bold as to make that suggestion? HR can have the reputation of being a cost-center that simply plans parties and pushes paper because of the people who practice the craft at a subpar level. If you find yourself unwilling to put in the time and effort to get better at what you do so that you can perform at a higher level for your employees and company, then it is time to ask yourself why.

I realize that what I am suggesting, bringing your best to deliver HR at the highest clip, is not for the faint of heart, and it takes an extraordinary person who can balance all of the corporate, political, and personal bullshit that comes with it. I cut through the crap and say, "Get out of HR" because having people who genuinely do not want to be in HR sets back employees, companies, and communities for years to come. I have seen bad HR firsthand and realize that the people who work at the company hate being there, the company loses money or does so in a cutthroat way, and the community suffers as the opportunity to make an impact is thwarted.

So, make that simple choice—find a vocation to which you can commit. It will set you free, and you will no longer perpetuate the stigma HR has been fighting for years. People, workplaces, and communities deserve more. They deserve much more. There is no way that you, as a leader in your organization, can expect someone to do something that you are not comfortable doing yourself. How can HR devise, plan, and lead an employee development program that HR is unwilling to live out independently? How can HR willingly hold others accountable and place employees who are struggling on a performance improvement plan if HR cannot hold itself to that same standard? As HR leaders, we must lead by example and show our principles through our actions. Show; don't just tell.

This reminds me of the one and only cop-out phrase my dad—a man of high integrity, great business success, and impeccable work ethic—used to say when I was a kid. "Do as I say, not as I do." I never understood this, and instead try to live by an "actions speak louder than words" mindset.

It is very simple to me. Grow or go!

Chapter 6
Do Your Job Well

If you follow the NFL, you are undoubtedly aware of Bill Belichick's coaching success. I'm sure it did not hurt to have the (arguably) greatest all-time NFL quarterback play for his team. Coach Belichick has a saying that now resonates around the NFL, into other professional sports and around high school and college athletics, and has even found its way into business. His directive is simple: do your job and do it well.

Once you are committed to growing your HR knowledge and making an impact on your employees, company, and community, make sure you do it at an elite rate. Why strive for anything less? The words "mediocre" or "average" are nowhere in the definitions of awesome or amazing, and amazingly awesome is what we are striving for.

Just for a moment, I want you to think about someone you know who does their job extremely well. What is it about them that stands out? I would guess that they take care of their business, remain professional, and are more than likable. They probably also go above and beyond for their colleagues, community, customers, and company.

Consider how you could improve by learning from someone who sets a high standard for themselves and those around them to achieve results. Take a quick moment to write down their name and make a point to reach out to them as soon as possible. Tell them that you recently reflected on the quality of their work and wanted to learn how they do what they do. Imagine the impact that your inquiry will have on that person. Plus, you get to learn a thing or two from them in the process.

In the meantime, I will break down the steps that it takes to do your job well, outlined here:

» Understand the needs of your people (employees, managers, executives, and shareholders).
» Understand the needs of your organization.
» Understand the potential impact you, your people, and your organization can have on the community.
» Develop a plan (we will cover this later).
» Identify the basics of your job.
» Set and communicate expectations.
» Do the basics well and consistently.
» Elevate to the next level once basics are consistently executed.
» Continuously improve all aspects of your business processes.

It is vital to understand all aspects of your job in order to do it well. Unfortunately, the job description that detailed the duties of your role when you were hired is likely out-of-date and needs to be refreshed. Start with a discovery process to better understand the needs of the people you serve, your organization, and the potential impact on the community.

After you complete this discovery, it is critical to boil down the information you have accumulated to the two or three most important parts of your role. For example, a payroll professional's priority is most likely to process payroll accurately. Then, ensure the department stays in compliance with federal, state, and local tax regulations. In addition, a payroll professional might determine that providing excellent customer service to the company's employees is a critical aspect of their job.

The basics of your job build the foundation for your *HR Like a Boss* plan.

Get Accountability by Seeking Buy-In

Once you have built your plan, I encourage you to take that plan to your CEO to get their feedback. Wait a second. Did I just suggest taking your plan to the CEO of your company and sharing it with them? Yes, I did, and you are probably thinking that I am crazy. I guess this idea is a little bit out there. The point of taking your plan to the CEO is to see if you believe enough in yourself and the idea of amazingly awesome HR to socialize an idea as bold as the one you are about to conjure up.

The rationale for my suggestion is as follows: achieving the next level of your career is going to take a ton of effort, time, energy, and support (especially from your CEO).

Before getting into the specifics of taking your plan to the CEO, it is important that you consider the politics, organizational mechanics, and any power struggles that exist within your company. Taking what could be a well-thought-out plan directly to your CEO without socializing the concepts with your peers and, most importantly, your direct supervisor may be the last thing you do at your company. I believe that the greatest ideas of any business come from within, not from the top. If your CEO is grounded and realistic, they know it too. However, any new, bold ideas you have should be vetted by you, your team, and your direct leader before marching into your CEO's office with a proclamation.

That said, some support for amazingly awesome HR must come from your CEO. If your CEO does not ultimately support you and your plan, then they more than likely do not support HR, and you need to know that. By taking your plan to the CEO or at the very least being able to make that ask, you are one step closer to doing *HR Like a Boss*. As someone who owns and loves what they do, nothing should get in your way, not even an unsupportive CEO.

Once you have scrutinized and vetted your plan within your close circle, I suggest making your plan, metrics, and goals very public. Tell as many people as you possibly can and garner their feedback. For me to write this book, I realized that I needed support and motivation. When I made the decision that I was going to do it, I initially told a close circle of friends and family. Then, I shared it with my entire team and many in my professional network. After that, I started to share my goal of writing a book on social media so the whole world would know about it. Why? Because I really wanted to get this project done and knew I would need the help and encouragement of others. I also knew that if I made my goal of writing a book public, I would not fail or let it slide. I strive to "do what I say and say what I do." It reminds me of the first agreement, "Be Impeccable with Your Word," in Don Miguel Ruiz's *The Four Agreements*.[1] If you say it, do it. Otherwise, people will not trust you. All of us have countless examples of those who let us down when their actions did not reflect their words. Don't get caught in that never-ending loop, or you may never get out.

Now that you know what the most important fundamentals of your job are, it is time that you execute and do them well. These items build upon your foundation to climb to the next level, so be a stickler on them. Then you can start to do things that might be cutting edge or in some respects transformative to your role, department, employees, culture, company, and community.

As you master the basics and start to build on them, it becomes evident that you need to measure your results and learn from this information. Do not wait for your manager or another executive to institute this measuring stick on you. Do it yourself! There is a reason they give you a scorecard before you go play a round of golf. By keeping track of how you are doing, you can see the progress that

1. Don Miguel Ruiz, *The Four Agreements* (San Rafael, CA: Amber-Allen Publishing, 1997).

you are making. Remember, we are looking for small and gradual improvements, which will take time and inevitably include setbacks and failures. That is 100 percent normal and part of the process.

As you start to glean insights from this data, you will see certain areas that need to be tweaked and adjusted. Getting better is an iterative process that takes time. Getting big results in a short period of time is a mirage for those who are not willing to persevere and put in the work.

Doing your job well is not always easy because doing the basics on a consistent basis is not sexy and will not be trending on social media. However, it will set you up for success and put you in a position to make a true impact on your career, employees, company, and community.

Careful What You Tell Yourself When Seeking Feedback

Thanks to the obsession with only showing every fun thing or great experience on social media and a society that awards participation trophies, people's ability to ask for and receive feedback has diminished. Why are we so afraid of constructive criticism? Learning to receive negative feedback is a direct path to improving oneself! As a continuation of doing your job well, someone who practices *HR Like a Boss* wants (and even needs) feedback from those they serve.

As an HR professional, you know that when people observe activity but are excluded from discussions, they often make up stories to fill in the blanks. These stories are often way worse than what's really going on!

The same goes for you when you seek feedback—I would say don't take it personally, but recognize at times it *can be* personal. Listen to the feedback and focus on what is said and how you can improve, not on your own "fill in the blanks" story.

Constructive criticism often triggers something inside that people have suppressed, struggled with, or haven't yet dealt with. For example, our constructive criticism of others could make them feel insecure or rejected, which is something they may have dealt with growing up. Therefore, many people tend to take feedback as a personal attack, as they link it to so many other internal issues. People also tend to give feedback a global meaning rather than viewing it as specific feedback on a particular instance.

Many of us put a tremendous amount of pressure and a greater-than-healthy degree of self-worth and identity into our job or career rather than in our family, personal interests, relationships, or faith. So constructive feedback can turn very personal for the recipient. They may feel both defensive and inadequate as a result. At the same time, too many others are not skilled at providing constructive criticism and end up attacking a person, not an issue. This can (and does) result in emotional responses to feedback.

Remember that every individual, and therefore every employee, is motivated differently and responds to different forms of motivation and recognition. Therefore, it is important to use the appropriate balance of praise, recognition, constructive feedback, and yes,

Figure 6–1. Don't forget that feedback is part of the communication loop.

even criticism. Balance is key. It is important to give as much energy to providing affirmation and positive feedback as needed in the form of constructive criticism. Effectively giving and receiving praise and providing feedback are set by the boundaries of the relationship with the person you are engaging in this dialogue. Not to mention, dialing into what motivates individuals will help chart the course for their development.

A salesperson may simply care about one thing: making money. That's not to paint salespeople as shallow but explains that many high-achieving salespeople receive self-worth from the size of their paycheck. That's not all salespeople, as I have known professionals with many different motivators. Even in sales, I had one high-functioning individual who derived more satisfaction from corporate recognition than the size of his paycheck.

That recognition is part of the psychological paycheck. In short, a psychological paycheck is what keeps you going to and happy at work. It can be a sense of belonging, feeling appreciated, or simply liking the flavor of coffee served. It's everything that cannot be quantified in a paycheck. All the thank-yous, attaboys, fist bumps, celebratory lunches with the head of your department, and corny plaques are part of a psychological paycheck as they let people know they are appreciated. These psychological paychecks should be included in your HR pillar of total rewards.

In appropriate balance, these deposits of recognition should build up a reserve of equity that allows someone to be in a positive place to ask for and receive feedback. Remember that statement as you step into a conversation that requires constructive feedback. Take an empathetic view as the other person combats the critical comments with defensiveness and harsh reactions. Their reaction is likely based on the fact that their bank of approving words and positive self-esteem is low on equity. Dig into that to understand.

Tana Mann Easton, the lead efficiency engineer at Focus to Evolve, has an interesting take on feedback: "Build relationships with employees that are predisposed to negative feedback. I like to think that positive feedback should outweigh negative feedback by a five to one ratio in order for negative feedback to land in a productive manner."

As someone who does (or seeks to do) *HR Like a Boss*, consider the status of your emotional balance on praise and recognition, knowing it will dictate your willingness to seek feedback or cause you to react negatively when given it. We cannot grow unless we hear how we are doing from those we serve. By making the person you are asking for feedback feel safe to share, you will be more likely to receive genuine feedback that you can use to improve everything you do. Safety is a cornerstone to creating transparency and honesty, but it can be difficult to create as employees often are concerned about sharing too much with someone from HR. Will it come back to haunt them? Can you be trusted? Building up this trust can take time and speaks to the importance of being a presence in your organization while developing those relationships.

Once a safe space is carefully established with employees, it is important to focus on empathetic listening. How you listen is critical. Put yourself in the shoes of the other person you are engaging in dialogue and try to understand their perspective and what they have experienced in the past that brings them to this conversation. Concentrate on truly listening. Close the door, shut off the smartphone, and silence your desk phone (if you still have one). Be prepared with a few questions and set expectations about what you are trying to accomplish from the very start. Then, let the conversation flow. Reinforce their sharing with thanks along the way and follow-up questions. Do not react or try to explain why things were the way they were. Just listen. As you seek feedback about yourself and your work, you are not there to win the argument or convince them otherwise about how they feel. Use the simple-to-say but difficult-to-do tactic of repeating back and use mirroring to ensure the person you are speaking with knows you hear them. This will help you understand how the person you are engaged in dialogue with feels about you, their work, and the function of HR.

Every single person in your life, at work or home, and even perfect strangers need to be and feel heard. There are two important steps to wrap up the discussion and ensure that you take in what the other intended for you to hear. First, you must repeat back some of the key points the person made to make certain that you understand precisely what they meant by their words. By doing so, you can validate that the two of you are on the same page and ensure clarity. Most importantly, assure the person that they are heard and they will likely leave feeling so. After giving yourself some time to reflect (let's say at least one hour and no more than twenty-four), it is essential to recap your discussion with an email. In that communication, commit to the items you own, then suggest how you will use the feedback to make positive changes. Then, you must make those changes and follow through with the people you received this feedback from. Otherwise, it is just blown air and a waste of time for you and most importantly the person who shared their feedback with you.

If you can perfect this method and do it repeatedly, you will build up tremendous credibility and trust. With that equity, you can show others how to gain feedback and help other employees ask and receive similar feedback. It is easier said than done not to take things personally, but doing so will serve you incredibly well in your journey to doing *HR Like a Boss*.

Have you ever quacked like a duck or barked like a dog in team training? If you said yes, you probably worked through some improvisational training about conflict and dispute resolution. If not, the tenets for improv are great for encouraging collaboration and accepting feedback. Brian Rolnick-Fox, an uncommon corporate educator combines experiential learning methodologies with improvisational theater. He had our team quacking, barking, dancing, and being machines while using the "yes and" mindset. Brian's unique learning solutions help teams achieve success while having tons of fun at the same time. We recently discussed seeking feedback and his philosophy on obtaining this valuable input.

"It's crucial to seek both formal and, perhaps more importantly, informal feedback. Seek feedback constantly and 'in the moment.' How are you reading the room? If you are already skilled at emotional intelligence, then great, but you need to develop your EQ if this is a challenge for you. You need to understand, 'What's my emotional state, what's the other person's emotional state, and what's the bridge between them?' Make sure you examine where the disconnect is even if it's in an offline, private setting."

Brian explained, "I like to ask employees and colleagues about their 'thoughts and feelings' because neuroscience tells us we tend to make decisions with our emotions and then look for logic that backs up our emotional decisions."

This conversation with Brian reminded me of and challenged the "it's not personal, it's business" badge of honor, or crock of shit, depending on your perspective. Often, it's cited as an excuse to brush off feelings in the business world, but the real world involves people with real feelings that guide their decisions and behavior. We can't divorce ourselves from the emotions that back most human decisions and behavior. It is best to acknowledge and live in those feelings while understanding and cataloging them as you progress to making those emotional connections.

By running toward the difficult and messy situations that come about every single day in corporate America, someone doing *HR Like a Boss* transcends the symptoms to appropriately explore and discover the root cause of the real issue. By effectively navigating through the feelings, emotions, critiques, and harsh words, more times than not, you will come out on the other end with enhanced clarity, a newfound trust, and mad respect, positioning you to move forward to your next challenge.

Chapter 7
Leverage Technology

When I think about HR technology, Tim Sackett immediately comes to mind. He is the most curiously passionate business leader and sought-after thought leader for all things HR tech. As a result of his expertise and dynamic view of HR, Tim was the very first guest on the *HR Like a Boss* podcast. Tim is a huge advocate for the HR profession and has authored countless blogs along with the SHRM-published book, *The Talent Fix: A Leader's Guide to Recruiting Great Talent.*

Be inspired by his poignant and direct comments (below) to be different by embracing your inner a tech-savvy HR pro.

> *The most lacking competency in HR leadership is technology, and it's not even close to the second one (which happens to be data). The problem is that technology is the one competency that sets great HR leaders apart from average HR leaders. When I sit down with C-suite teams and there is an HR executive in the room who truly understands technology for their function, they are viewed in a completely different and positive way by all the other executives. Immediately, you feel the trust from the other executives that this person has HR under control. That doesn't mean the HR executive needs to know how to code or program, but they need to be keenly*

aware of what their HR technology can do and not do and, if needed, whether there is additional HR technology available in the market that can do what is needed.

Clearly, one of the best ways to stand out and make life easier for any business professional, including HR professionals, is to leverage technology. The keyword in that sentence is "leverage." Someone doing *HR Like a Boss* doesn't just *use* HR technology. Instead, they take advantage of it to maximize their capabilities. Unfortunately, the opposite outcome can happen when trying to leverage technology turns into a disaster. Nothing is worse and more negatively impactful than a failed implementation of new technology or missing the mark by selecting the wrong vendor partner despite good intentions. You don't want technology to be a hindrance, and I have seen both positive and negative outcomes with the use of HR technology throughout my career.

As cloud-based, software as a service (SaaS), and artificial intelligence (AI) technologies have evolved and now dominate the marketplace, the workload and responsibilities for the generalist HR community have grown exponentially, so much so that the Society for Human Resource Management (SHRM) and its local chapters are building out special interest groups to educate the HR generalist population on technologies, trends, and best practices. Furthermore, niche associations like the International Association for Human Resource Information Management (IHRIM) and its chapters are folding. Over time, the responsibilities for maintaining and advancing an organization's HR technology have shifted from technical professionals in HR (like human resources information system managers and human capital management analysts) to HR pros who have other functional responsibilities. As Tim encourages, "become a super-user for your HR technology before making HR technology decisions. It's only when you fully utilize the system that you'll understand the features and gaps."

For some additional context, since starting my career with ADP, I have worked on nearly a thousand projects that had something to do with HR technology or business process improvement. In these projects, clients were trying to optimize their existing HR technology or business processes, implement a new system, or identify a new vendor after becoming disenchanted with their current HR technology or service provider.

Looking back on those projects and experiences, it is incredible how many things have changed while so much has remained the same. To help you stand out by better leveraging your HR technology, consider these factors that have remained relatively constant (going back as far as the nineties, which dates me and the start of my career).

First, a dichotomy exists between what clients expect and receive from their HR technology service providers. Ultimately, this is an indictment of both parties, as it is the responsibility of the buyer to vet and understand the capabilities and offerings of the HR technology. Throughout my entire career, I've learned clients expect more than what many providers can deliver. Clients must understand *exactly* what their HR technology is and is not capable of. Each HR technology provider has its niche. For some, their differentiator is workforce management. For others, it is payroll or talent management. There simply isn't an HR technology or service provider that can do it all exceptionally well. It would be ideal to have a single platform that does it all amazingly awesomely, but not one HR technology provider has invested the resources to crack the code of building a world-class platform that brings you uniformity and expertise from application to retirement. Based on this, it seems likely technology will continue to improve to address the client's needs.

Do not get me wrong, HR technology providers have developed countless innovations over the years and expanded the capabilities of their systems beyond what we ever thought was possible. To provide some perspective, there was a time when it was a big deal that an employee's HR record linked to their payroll record.

In the constant innovation and expansion of HR technology lies the root cause of the problem. The pace at which new technology is being developed and folded into existing programs can be euphorically beneficial but also complex and downright overwhelming for the generalist population to absorb. It is nearly impossible for human resources professionals (the number of which are diminishing in many companies) to consume and leverage the providers' robust and vast systems.

Meanwhile, HR technology providers are incentivized to increase their market share and drive up the price per employee per month (PEPM) to generate revenue and shareholder value. So, as HR technology innovators attempt to create a uniform nexus among the wide, ever-expanding range of modules, services, and offerings, they dilute the user experience as the amount of responsibility and diversity of content unintentionally overwhelms those who consume it.

Another aspect that has not changed much over the years is just how consequential payroll is in any HR technology system implementation or optimization project. Despite advancements in artificial intelligence, implementing new systems is still labor-intensive, stressful, and difficult to do effectively. The main culprit is payroll. In many cases, too many organizations overlook the importance of the payroll function. In other cases, organizations and employees forget about payroll apart from nuisance frustrations that consumers experience when there is a mistake. Payroll is *way* more complex than just pressing the payroll button. Far too often, the payroll department or leader is not even involved in the decision-making team when it comes to selecting, implementing, and optimizing HR technology.

Beyond payroll, we often see other critical functional areas, like workforce management and benefits administration, overlooked. Effectively implementing a workforce management system with labor forecasting, employee productivity, time and attendance, PTO management, workflow, and automation takes tremendous planning, time, and resources. It is not an add-on module that can be easily implemented in a few short weeks. Benefits management and administration also often get lost in the wash as the complexity of integrating the benefits process and systems with the HR technology and various carriers is underestimated. The timing of open enrollment can creep up on the implementation teams who are busy configuring the core HR application or testing the conversion of payroll data. On top of that, an abundance of standalone and integrated technology and service solutions are available in the workforce management and benefits marketplace.

As a result of the abundance of functionality in HR technology, the complexity associated with successfully deploying and leveraging it, and the frequent lack of oversight to thoroughly review the most challenging aspects of an HR technology implementation or optimization, we continue to see employers and teams underestimate the amount of effort, time, and resource capacity required to effectively plan, learn, use, and optimize their HR technology.

My bet is the first time you participate in an HR and payroll technology implementation, it won't go smoothly. Much like buying your first house, you might not be sure of the exact process to follow, and it can be overwhelming. However, with each implementation (or new house), you'll learn a bit more. A lot of it comes down to experience and having a handle on project management. If you're at a larger company, look to leverage expertise in your IT and finance departments. For practitioners at smaller companies, look to your network to ask for advice or find a consultant who can help you.

Over time, the responsibility falls squarely on the clients' shoulders to optimize and transform the use of their HR technology. Still, HR continues to rely too heavily on providers to transform their business before the proper and thorough use of their technology. This creates a perpetual wheel of thinking that the problem lies with their HR software or payroll service when the ownership of success or failure ultimately rests on the client and its HR, payroll, benefits, compensation, recruiting, IT, and finance teams. Don't waste your time or energy pointing the finger anywhere but at you and your team.

There is a reason that the phrase "buyer beware" exists. To be successful and grow, HR technology providers must deliver a profit to their shareholders while developing technology, innovating solutions, and providing world-class service (at scale). All of which, by the way, is really expensive and highly complex to pull off. As a result, a standard set of technology and services offered by the providers must accommodate a large volume of customers. The only reason you can afford an off-the-shelf technology is because tens of thousands of clients are sharing in the investments and expenses associated with developing the software.

In many cases, the software providers do many things really well. At the same time, they have been forced to expand their product and service offerings to curtail competitive pressures as they look to differentiate themselves in the marketplace and grow their market share. Ultimately, it is up to the client to understand how to make the technology and services work for their own particular use.

To continue our examination of the HR technology landscape, let's explore what has shifted with the HR technology providers. Spoiler alert: it's changed certain aspects of the job description for HR professionals.

The first aspect of the landscape that has changed is the number of providers, which has drastically expanded from manageable to overwhelming. It is estimated that there are over twenty thousand different HR technology vendors, and every year that number seems to expand with innovations and niche providers. Just think about that for one moment. If you are struggling with your incumbent software provider, how do you figure out which of the other 19,999 HR technology vendors would solve the problems and challenges you face? We will get to that point at the end of this section.

In addition to an increased number of providers, established providers have drastically expanded their offerings. Now they have expanded modules, new service offerings, integrations, survey tools, partnerships, and are experimenting with augmented and virtual reality. In short order, these new enhancements will become the standard, and new solutions and inventions will further broaden the technology stack and offerings available in the marketplace.

We have seen the evolution of how information is passed between systems thanks to companies like Joynd, Zapier, and Dell Boomi. In the past, interfaces between one system were complex and costly and required extensive development and testing. Application programming interfaces (APIs) have been developed to connect multiple software applications in a more efficient and cost-effective way so that data can "seamlessly" pass through various systems. I put the word "seamlessly" in quotes for a reason. You might still run into data mapping errors or systems that seem to speak different languages. It's for this reason that two of the biggest sticking points in a new system implementation can be data conversion and validation. You can run into simple issues where one system uses "email" and another uses "e-mail." This minute difference might not seem big, but it could keep all your employees' emails from being shared between systems properly. Also, some systems require certain fields, but others do not. This could keep thousands of records from transferring.

I have been around HR technology my entire business career, but please do not confuse me with a technical resource. With that perspective, this aspect of technology has expanded tremendously, making it way easier for any company to connect their HR, payroll, ERP, accounting, and website technologies together.

As previously mentioned, HR professionals are being asked to do more with less: less time, less human capital, and so on. The effective use of HR technology can help eliminate manual processes, automate time-consuming workflows, and help employees find answers to questions through self-service tools. As HR pros look to leverage their HR technology, they need the support of their technology service provider. Over the years, the service relationship between HR and vendors has become tense. Complex ticketing systems, triage service models, and specialized support have caused HR end users to become frustrated by the service they receive from the vendor. At the same time, as vendor technologies offer more and more modules, services, and so on, it becomes nearly impossible for a customer service representative to keep up with all of the components, bells and whistles, and added features of their own product!

Customer service reps are not experts on all aspects of the system they serve, and instead are, as my dad would say, "Jack of all trades, master of none." So, when a client calls to address an issue, they may bounce around the service loop and become frustrated that no one can immediately address the issue at hand. We all know what it feels like when we call any service company for support and cannot get an adequate resolution or answer.

Another unique development in the HR technology landscape is the evolution of human capital management (HCM) technology infrastructure. Many new technology providers have developed an all-in-one system with a consistent look and feel and a single rules engine running throughout, from recruiting to payroll to reporting. In comparison, others offer a unified solution that provides fully developed functionality by acquiring or assimilating multiple technologies and service offerings. Further still, other providers offer a best-of-breed point solution, and partner with other point systems and full-suite HCMs through integration to meet specific client needs. Doing *HR Like a Boss* means knowing the nuances between certain systems. You need to know their differences in terms of look, feel, and process. Someone doing *HR Like a Boss* looks at the big picture and chooses the best infrastructure to meet the organization's strategic needs. Finally, they understand that no one technology can be best-in-breed across all areas of the employee life cycle and is able to set priorities that align with the overall vision of the organization.

While unified HR technologies can have robust capabilities across a wide range of tasks from job application to retirement, each platform is better at certain aspects based on its genesis. All systems started somewhere. As a result, the unified technologies may be an industry leader in one or two aspects like workforce management or payroll, but may lag in other functional elements. Educate yourself and be prepared for your technology's strengths and weaknesses.

If you're not ready for the inevitable pushback that comes with all change, providers are often the fall guy for the growing pains of any technology deployment. If technology and change aren't managed, you find yourself switching from one tech solution to another as often as you turn over the thirty-nine-month lease on your car. Simply changing technologies without careful consideration of process improvement, standardization, and modernization will likely not improve your service relationship. Instead, you will grow tired of getting similar results after going through the pain and suffering that can exist when switching from one provider to another. Accounts payable might issue a check to another vendor, but the problems remain the same.

Steps to Follow

To avoid these pitfalls, someone doing *HR Like a Boss* follows these steps with their current technology before even considering making a change, going to market, or implementing a new system:

Strategize

Precisely define what you want your technology stack to look like and how to best leverage it within your company. This is a "close your eyes and imagine what you want it to be" exercise. Do not cloud your judgment and limit yourself with your current environment!

Assess

Take the time to examine the current state of your tech stack thoroughly. Consider hiring an unbiased resource who has subject matter expertise in your existing systems. Develop a current state and future state visual of your environment.

Plan

Once your discovery process and assessments are complete, it is time to plan your priorities, timing, resources, module deployment, self-service, and so on.

Train

Once you're committed to an HR technology platform, your entire team must complete the available and often free training on your application. It is amazing how many clients have not taken advantage of the training opportunities. Once you have completed your training, find online and in-person user group communities.

Standardize

Wherever you can, standardize your business practices across your various business entities and companies. For example, look to create uniformity with aspects of your business like pay codes, work rules, earnings, deductions, pay dates, and pay periods.

Stabilize

It is of utmost importance to create a solid foundation ensuring your basic modules are stabilized, especially payroll, core HR, benefits, and workforce management. You and your team are prepared to optimize your HR technology by creating this solid footing.

Optimize

Once your system is on solid footing, you are ready to optimize the tool and take advantage of some of the bells and whistles that may be the exact reasons you selected the system. Taking a strategic approach and developing an optimization project plan to ensure everyone within your organization is on the same page will increase your chances of truly enhancing your system. Carefully consider items like the availability of resources, other strategic initiatives, competing projects, and PTO schedules to set up your team to optimize your HR technology fully.

Partner

The idea of partnering with your provider has become a lost art. It is most likely attributed to the turnover within the corporate world and within vendor partners. No matter what, it is critical to develop a personal rapport and relationship with multiple players at your provider company. It is suggested that you develop a positive working relationship with your sales representative, relationship manager, customer service manager, and one or two executive leaders. When an issue arises or the vendor does not deliver on their end of the bargain, you can quickly connect with those you have developed a relationship with instead of scrambling to figure out who you should call. Not to mention, it will help you in your negotiations on future contract extensions and purchasing new services from your HR technology provider.

Document

Documenting might seem like a mundane step in the process, but it is paramount to complete it throughout your use of your HR technology. Taking the time to document the steps needed to conduct critical business practices like onboarding, payroll, and offboarding will pay major dividends. It will allow you to truly understand every aspect of a particular process and shine a light on the inefficient, antiquated, and redundant areas. Not to mention, it will create a reference if an important employee is out, and a backup resource is required to complete a task.

Transform

The work you have done building out self-service, workflows, sequences, next-level modules, and system automation has put you at a point to truly leverage your HR technology and change the way you do business. You are now in a position to implement some machine learning, AI, surveying tools, and analytical gadgets that can help make your HR technology a differentiator for your organization.

Build Your Tech Stack

Someone doing *HR Like a Boss* intentionally and carefully takes steps to leverage technology to get out of the mundane and often antiquated tasks that haunt and hold back the HR profession. By taking the time to build an HR tech stack that you can use to your advantage, you will gain more time each day to focus on the strategic initiatives. Use this time to prioritize how you can drive results and positive change for your employees and organization.

Chapter 8
Manage Distractions

A big part of doing *HR Like a Boss* includes focusing on the *big picture* and not letting little things get in the way of being awesome! Distractions stop the most well-intentioned from making an impact.

I started a 100 percent virtual business in 2010 that had many traditional business owners and leaders scratching their heads. They questioned the validity and potential of Willory's business model, and many were skeptical about the long-term viability of our firm because we relied on work-from-home employees. Imagine my audacity! Fast-forward to today, and we've received countless calls and consulting engagements to strategize on taking a traditional business to 100 percent virtual. During the pandemic, I was featured on podcasts, special webinars, and presentations to share with the rest of the world the best practices in 2020. My calendar was jammed with requests as the world faced our new virtual, work-from-home, remote, whatever you want to call it reality.

When asked how and why I started a 100 percent virtual business, I focused on the why: my family.

In the months leading up to starting Willory, my wife had just given birth to our second child, Mallory, and I took one month to work from home to help get everyone in my home settled with the new arrival. When I had time to work, I was fascinated by how much I could get done while not being distracted with the numerous casual conversations, lunchtime breaks, and water cooler conversations you experience in an office. I could get a ton of work done and be right there if a diaper needed changing or to share a meal with my two-year-old son. After a month, I returned to my traditional office setting and quickly began to feel like I was missing out on something at home. My wife would tell me about their day. Some might think only little things happened when I was gone, but I was missing big-deal milestones such as first sounds, funny looks, and first steps. I powered through but finally came to realize that I could not sustain working in an office while missing out on over forty hours per week of my family growing up.

I had to figure this out. How could I have the best of both worlds? I hatched a plan and approached my wife. Her jaw dropped when I said I wanted to leave my executive search firm. She quickly reminded me that she was on leave from her position as a part-time adjunct professor at the University of Akron and gave me a reality check, reminding me that I was responsible for providing for our family. I reluctantly returned to my traditional office setting but was still determined to figure this out. My longing to be there for my family while building my business was the riddle I had to solve.

About six months after my daughter was born, I figured it out. I had saved up about $50,000 to cover our family expenses while I had no income and invested in starting my business, Willory, which I named after my son, Will, and daughter, Mallory. Willory would be focused on serving the HR and payroll community (which no one was doing in our community as far as I could see). I promised my wife that if I ran out of money in my business, I would go back into corporate America and get a sales position (which I was confident I could secure). My plan was compelling, and my wife, Emily, has always supported my business ventures. When I got the green light, there was *no way* that I was going to fail and go back to working for someone else.

With this focus on my family, I zeroed in on being as productive as possible and found that limiting the typical distractions that come

Figure 8–1. Caricature of Emily, Will, Mallory, and John Bernatovicz

with a traditional office setting caused my productivity to skyrocket. It was clear to me that I got more done when I wasn't distracted. I had never realized the number of diversions that existed in a traditional office setting.

So Many Stimuli . . . Only One You

Now that my personal backstory on the impact of managing distractions is out of the way, let's dive into how you can become more productive by managing distractions and showcasing this discipline to your company's employees. In this instance, we are not talking about HR's responsibility to ensure the masses are productive by managing employee distractions and blocking websites and social media. Businesspeople have countless stimuli that can distract them from their job. While LinkedIn, ESPN, and other websites can be distractions, I am not suggesting policing employees for taking a five-minute break to check their fantasy football team or checking out the latest gossip on TMZ. Rather, organizations do a great job creating workplace distractions without the web's assistance. Let's look at the two biggest culprits of sucking away productivity: meetings and email.

These culprits are profoundly ingrained into the workplace. It's not uncommon for meetings and emails to distract you from completing the basic priorities of your job, leaving you with no time to perform in a way that would prompt you to feel like you are doing *HR Like a Boss*.

This means you must not only learn how to manage distractions but exemplify this behavior, leading to the opportunity to teach others to do the same. Find ways to do your own job in a highly productive manner, then relay that knowledge to your organization's leaders who can pass along these behaviors to their people, creating an amazingly high-productive, high-functioning business filled with *bosses*.

To make that kind of change, it is often necessary to look at the realities of the time and productivity you might speculate is lost through meetings and email. You may not have the organizational data to determine the true impact, but taking the time to assess these realities could lead to beneficial changes at your organization.

From an HR perspective, one of your primary responsibilities is to serve the needs of your employees and help them to perform at their personal best. In doing so, it is critical to remove the barriers your employees experience that get in the way of their success. To get a sense of how meetings and emails impact employee productivity, survey your organization to learn the time spent attending meetings and checking emails and the impact it has on their ability to do their job effectively. Then, establish a small focus group of willing employees to shadow and monitor their actual time spent on meetings and emails.

Once you have this organization-specific data, share the facts with your leadership team, analyze the information, and develop a plan. The plan should center on helping your employees shed the unproductive habits associated with meetings and emails and better leverage these engrained parts of work life to be productive resources, not time-sucking monsters.

Meetings Like a Boss

Speaking of scary things, have you ever had a meeting without an agenda or clear purpose, and therefore nothing productive was accomplished? Talk about a waste of time. If you can make meetings productive and efficient, think about the hero you will become. This is a prevailing challenge that most employers face. The immediate impact is an employee's lack of time to complete their primary job responsibilities when they're in meetings all day.

Someone doing *HR Like a Boss* makes the dream of productive meetings a reality. In some respects, it is quite simple:

»   Establish an agenda.
»   Only invite those who need to attend.
»   Stick to the agenda and timeline.
»   Assign a proctor to manage distractions and document next steps.
»   Develop a follow-up plan to make sure things get done.
»   Don't forget to take notes (and review those notes before the next meeting).

If you're going to do *HR Like a Boss*, meetings will be less frequent, more structured, and much more disciplined. Meetings will have a purpose along with a defined beginning and end. Some other things to keep in mind when doing *HR Like a Boss* with meetings include the following:

»   Stop multitasking and don't let attendees do it either. If everyone focuses on the meeting's objective and only the meeting's objective, you'll find a one-hour meeting may take 30 or 45 minutes.

» Manage the meeting to the clock. If a meeting is supposed to be 30 minutes, it's the boss's job to keep the meeting on track and finish on time. This often requires following allotted time for specific agenda items.

» Rate the effectiveness of your meetings at the conclusion to learn what did and did not work well.

Considering this book's premise is that *anyone* can do *HR Like a Boss*, let's examine boss-behaviors for meeting attendees versus meeting organizers. How can someone be a boss when they are not a boss in terms of meetings?

If you find yourself in conflict with a specific meeting scheduled by your direct boss, make sure you take control of your own time (like a boss). Explain to your boss the conflict, why the conflict is important, and ask to participate only in the parts of the meeting where your insight and counsel are most needed. Additionally, ask for someone to take notes for this part of the meeting or record it (check to ensure you comply with recording regulations), as Microsoft Teams and Zoom make recording your meeting so very easy. A quick side note: make sure everyone is aware the meeting is being recorded. It will likely minimize the bantering that can exist in meetings while preventing someone from making a bone-headed, lacking-self-awareness comment. Or so one can hope.

Email Is Your Friend

Now that we have eradicated the unproductive meeting from your organization, let's bring out our best MacGyver skills to right the wrongs of email. The concept of electronic messaging started when Neil Papworth, a British test engineer, used his personal computer to send a message via the Vodafone network to wish "Merry Christmas" to his friend Richard Jarvis in 1992—thus, the world received another communication innovation.

As we referenced earlier, have you ever had a colleague, peer, or friend tell you that they are so busy doing everything else that they do not have time to get their real job done? Well, it can absolutely be true. An overflowing email inbox is a real distraction that causes all of us to get pulled away from our real work. Couple that with the fact that it can take a long time to get back into the work we should be performing when we get distracted.

Employees are being robbed of a large portion of their day by unproductive matters. Email can single-handedly distract someone from doing *HR Like a Boss*. Instead, use email to your advantage by using out-of-office notifications, managing your inbox down to zero daily, and leveraging tasks to ensure you are staying organized so you can prioritize what truly needs to get done. Let's lead by example and not be a slave to our inbox, but instead focus on more productive, proactive behaviors.

People often feel internal pressure to answer emails in a timely fashion. Doing *HR Like a Boss*, however, recognizes that immediate responses to emails don't necessarily contribute to the company's bottom line. Setting expectations about the timing of your follow-up while managing your inbox to zero unread messages on your terms exemplifies what it means to do *HR Like a Boss*.

Remember Tana Mann Easton, the lead efficiency engineer at Focus to Evolve? She teaches professionals to use their inbox as a friend, not foe: "Professionals can use email systems as a second brain that helps them live the life they want to live." Tana's recommendations for email management offer excellent guidance for managing distractions and include "turning off the default and distracting email notifications."

Her tips stress operating with an empty inbox: "The less email you have in your inbox, the more bandwidth you have to think and perform. Ideally, you should be able to get to zero emails in your inbox."

I will admit that managing the distraction of my email is one of the hardest things for me to achieve. Email is the continuous dopamine hit for someone like me with a short attention span, and I must consciously work the temptation out of my mind. I tell myself that I get more emails than most, and I find email very distracting. So, I only address the most critical messages. I hired Tana to help me get to an empty email inbox, prioritize the most essential tasks, become more organized, and control my time. This has been and will continue to be a lifelong struggle for me, but I understand the impact of getting it under control so that it does not distract me from the most important tasks.

Over time, I have discovered that my inbox and daily metrics go hand in hand; the lower my unread messages, the lower my productivity, as reflected by our analytics. To maximize my efficiency, I've made a conscious effort to dedicate blocks of time to certain tasks. I ignore email during those blocks of time that I have set aside to get the most important things done. I have found that frequently switching over to my email inbox disrupts my concentration and ability to do meaningful work.

Our brain sends bursts of dopamine when we see those email pop-ups indicating a new message or when your phone buzzes to indicate a mysterious and unread message, making it incredibly hard to ignore and change the course of your day. As Tana suggests, disable email alerts and notifications (on your phone and computer), flip your phone over, turn it on silent, or even go as far as uninstalling your work email app.

HR Like a Boss means getting past the need to check and respond to emails immediately so you can focus on more important, key priorities.

For example, doing *HR Like a Boss* in a manufacturing environment means taking time to walk the floor and interact with employees. You must do that without being "half present" because of the addiction to checking email via your smartphone. Pay attention to your main objective, and if something needs to be addressed, excuse yourself for a quick moment and take care of it so you can return to focus on the task at hand. Sometimes I find myself in meetings or on calls, and something needs to be addressed immediately. Rather than trying to do two things at once, I excuse myself for one minute, take care of the emergency, and fully re-engage with an apology.

Don't forget that managing email goes both ways. You shouldn't cc, bcc, or include people who do not absolutely need to be in the email chain. Also, your smartphone can make phone calls. Yes, it seems inconvenient at the time, but a ten-minute call can find a resolution much faster than a multiple response email chain ever could. At Willory, we have an informal rule that if an email chain goes on for more than three responses, it warrants a live conversation.

Time after Time Management

Now that we have considered the time-sucking facts and devised a plan to be more effective with meetings and email, let's continue your diligence in owning your time. Don't let others control your time, but instead take control of your schedule.

No matter where you are on the org chart, a boss learns how to own their schedule.

Tana Mann shared that "we are architects of our time. Every minute of the day is your minute, so use your calendar for personally and professionally important things to you, from spending time with family to exercising and dominating your work time with important activities that will make a positive impact on your employees and business. This allows you to utilize your calendar to measure how much time you have available each day. Be the architect of your own time and manage your minutes."

Tana also suggests that HR help organizations by instituting time management training. She points out that while we assume professionals have organizational skills, the reality is that human nature leads to us living our days by "simply reacting to the latest email in our inbox or complaint."

"Nine out of ten professionals I see are simply bad at time management," explained Tana. "In today's work environment, far too many people worship at the altar of busy-ness. Being busy isn't the same as being effective!" By doing *HR Like a Boss,* you can help your organization re-examine how your company improves its productivity. Minimizing and managing distractions is a profound step in that direction. Set proper expectations and suggestions around the time spent emailing and consider more efficient alternatives.

Alter, for the better, your company's meeting practices and lead a paradigm shift away from the assumption that being in meetings equals being effective as opposed to busy.

Let's end this section with a reminder to walk the walk before talking the talk. People are paying attention. When they see you doing *HR Like a Boss* and managing your time and distractions, employees will flock to you to understand your tricks and processes to master time efficiency, become highly productive, and minimize the negative impact of distractions. Someone doing *HR Like a Boss* avoids and minimizes distractions. You must be laser-focused and engaged to help your employees grow and business flourish.

Part IV
Be Better

Chapter 9
Keen Focus on Talent

During my journey of writing this book, I have had the amazing fortune to speak with countless business leaders and HR professionals on the *HR Like a Boss* podcast and in a wide array of other forums. Along the way, I discussed my book with Nickie DiCarlo, and we dove into some detail about the chapter titles and sections that make up *HR Like a Boss*. Nickie brings a politeness to her contrarian thought that has served her incredibly well in her HR consulting practice.

Thinking differently is critical to looking at the existing opportunities that HR has faced for years and solving the new problems and challenges that an HR pro deals with daily. To Nickie's point, critical thought is simply not enough. On top of thinking differently, we must be different. It's HR's job to take action on new ideas, strategies, and tactics so we can deliver meaningful and impactful change to our employees, company, and community.

In this section, we dive into what it takes to be better. Those doing *HR Like a Boss* focus their time and efforts to drive results for all stakeholders. To me and many other business professionals, HR is synonymous with talent acquisition, and the idea of being better starts with the people you work with every day. Their abilities and inabilities are a direct reflection of the HR department. HR is in the driver's seat, with the capability to bring real change and help your company deliver results by acquiring and developing the right talent. Being different starts with *everyone* in HR and ultimately every employee in your organization running toward helping your organization attract and retain top talent. This chapter is for my fellow HR peers who struggle with talent acquisition or who run away from recruiting. It takes a collective effort to improve your organization's ability to acquire top talent. There are no excuses, just opportunities to show off HR's impact on making a bottom-line difference while helping connect the right people to your organization.

HR has a tremendous influence on leaders and managers. All too often, the basics of solid leadership and accountability are overlooked. As a result, employees leave in droves because of a poor relationship with a manager or a lack of respect for their leadership style. Who do we blame for that? No one. It is simply another opportunity for HR to spread its wings and showcase your ability to drive real change by intentionally developing your leaders. By helping managers be transparent with their communication, you will decrease turnover and drive employee engagement through the roof.

In the process, the relationships you establish with your managers will become lifelong as you hone their managerial skills. By taking a genuine interest in their development and helping them by improving your own communication skills and ability to deal in the gray, work will transcend beyond what happens during your regular nine-to-five. If you cannot tell, I believe that better HR leads to more engaged employees and profitable businesses, resulting in a better world. Let's put *HR Like a Boss* into action and be better . . . starting right *now*!

Within an organization, the most widely known functional area that falls within HR's responsibilities and directly impacts the outcomes of the business is talent acquisition.

To see the impact that talent acquisition and development can have on an organization, we (especially those from the 'Land) do not have to look much further than a miserable twenty-year stretch (1999 to 2018) by my beloved Cleveland Browns football team. After being reinstituted into the National Football League (NFL) following Art Modell's fateful move that snatched Cleveland's beloved football franchise right out of the hands of diehard fans, the Browns had the worst record in the NFL, winning less than one third of their games. During those miserable two decades, the Browns only had a winning record in three seasons, and they mustered only one playoff appearance, during which they lost their only playoff game in those 20 years to their archrival, the Pittsburgh Steelers. In addition, in 2018, they joined the 2008 Detroit Lions as the only NFL team to have a winless season at a dreadful 0–16. In this time, the Browns had two ownership groups, nine different general managers, ten head coaches, and an astonishing thirty-two starting quarterbacks. During the same time frame, the New England Patriots had one coach, Bill Belichick, and five starting quarterbacks, with Tom Brady starting 93 percent of games during this same twenty-year stretch. As a result, the Patriots won six Super Bowl titles during that same timeline.

The primary reason for the Browns' dismal results over this prolonged period was their historic ineptness to acquire the right talent and their shortcomings in developing the talent they did have. For nearly twenty years, the Browns' leadership repeatedly missed on first-round draft picks, with the most infamous mistake being drafting Johnny "Football" Manziel. Each blundering misstep on first-round picks not only hurt the team, but poor talent acquisition actually set the franchise back.

HR's top-of-the-list responsibility is to, in a socially responsible manner, have the right people in the right place at the right time and unleash their full potential to the mutual benefit of all stakeholders in the business. Millions of other stories in business, sports, movies, art, and education support this simple idea. Good talent (that is developed) wins and bad talent (that is not developed) loses.

Learn to Like It

If talent acquisition is so important and foundational, then why do so many organizations struggle, just like the Cleveland Browns, to attract, develop, and retain top talent? I've seen countless HR professionals who lack the commitment to drive positive and impactful results when it comes to talent acquisition and development. I have also spoken to countless HR professionals, and they have said (and I am paraphrasing for effect and to amalgamate hundreds of similar comments), "I don't do recruiting because I don't like it." What? I don't like to sleep as it takes away from my twenty-four-hour-a-day productivity . . . but it is critical to my survival!

Having heard "I don't like recruiting" far too often, my response is that recruiting is *everyone's* responsibility. HR needs to model this behavior (and take responsibility) to ensure everyone in the organization is striving to bring in new, top talent while adopting a family-like mentality to take care of our own when it comes to development and retention. This lack of commitment, combined with the absence of a clear and organization-wide talent strategy, causes many organizations to flounder as they rely on a "post and hope" recruiting strategy along with a "sink or swim" approach for employee development.

Look in the mirror and have a personal heart-to-heart discussion about your focus and how you're stepping up your talent acquisition game to make it your primary priority. By doing so, you will be far more equipped to build an effective talent acquisition and development strategy, one that has been well-thought-out and thoroughly vetted and eventually agreed upon and tweaked year over year by your leadership team and managers. Your talent acquisition and development strategy must include the following

» Your cultural makeup and core values;
» Diversity, equity, inclusion, and belonging guideposts;

» A clear brand message to the candidate community;

» Influential people to execute on this strategy, including those who own and support this plan;

» Optimized talent acquisition technologies and systems;

» Defined and documented processes that will support your strategy;

» A plan for how you will organize and optimize your efforts;

» Your sourcing strategy;

» A process to ensure that your hiring, onboarding, and development process delivers for your purpose-driven, impact-making team; and

» A deep understanding of

› the strategy, objectives, and goals of the business, including its purpose, values, and culture, and

› how the business makes money and what skills are needed so the business can reach its goals now and in the future.

Once you have your talent acquisition and development strategy plan, it is time to operationalize it like a boss. It takes two different mindsets and at times a drastically different set of tools to develop the strategy than it does to deliver on it. Implementing your plan requires pulling a team together through roles, responsibilities, goals, and recurring department meetings.

Aspire to perfect the basic activities that make up your priorities. You should have at least one and no more than three key priorities and the outcomes you desire from these priorities in your plan. For example, some talent acquisition and development priorities are hiring for culture and core values, serving hiring managers, improving the candidate experience, unifying a training program for the entire organization, and developing succession plans. Talent acquisition teams measure turnover, time to fill, employee engagement, hire quality, candidate experience, productivity, and other recruiting-related outcomes.

Show Your Work (Value)

Be mindful that one of the knocks by nonbelievers of HR is the lack of a concrete measurement of the impact of HR on the bottom line. As they say, don't hate the player; hate the game. So, there is no need to blame the nonbelievers. Instead, create your plan, simplify it through your priorities, and create objective and subjective measures that will determine your progress and the ultimate success or failure of your plan. Failure is a strong word, especially as our path is always iterative and requires ample time to truly see the impact of a well-thought-out strategy. So, if the talent acquisition and development plan for a given year does not work, retool it, learn from your mistakes, and make it better.

Speaking of ambiguous measurements, quality of hire is one of the most effective but customizable metrics in the talent acquisition space. Quality of hire indicates the effectiveness of a hiring process and is intended to measure the impact on the business of new hires. The funny part is that a wide array of variables can be used to calculate this metric. So, each talent acquisition team can develop the most critical factors to include in a quality of hire measurement. For example, employee performance, length of employment, employee engagement, time to fill, core values alignment, and hiring manager satisfaction are all factors that could be used in calculating quality of hire. Ideally, utilize a talent intelligence system that leverages AI technology in each stage of the employee life cycle.

If you are not measuring quality of hire, I would recommend spending time in your talent acquisition and development planning sessions to identify the three or four key indicators that your HR and leadership team define as indicative of a quality hire. Then, develop a uniform measurement or scale for those factors. Once you have your formula, go back in time and look at all new hires in the last two to three years and plug their data into your formula. Creating a baseline helps you know where to improve and empowers you to interpret your scores on a semiannual or annual basis.

Improve the Candidate Experience

Another critical talent acquisition metric that profoundly impacts company performance is candidate experience. This looks at your community's impression of your company throughout all aspects of the candidate life cycle. Why is candidate experience so necessary to business results? Simply put, a great candidate experience can lead to a new hire and potential advocate for your company and its products. Conversely, a poor candidate experience will produce a community of company detractors that results in negative feelings toward your company's brand and products. This will undoubtedly drive down sales and profitability. Happy candidates equal better results.

For now, the easiest way to think about improving your candidate experience is to put yourself in the shoes of your candidates and live the experience of your hiring process. Be empathetic and respectful and consider their perspective. Curtail the aspects of your hiring process that could lead to disenchanted candidates and improve the hiring process with better candidate communication, including clearly defined expectations and timelines for your candidates during the interview process, and live up to the standards you set.

So, how do you build a great plan that drives quality hires and amazing candidate experiences? One unique and potentially thought-provoking point to contemplate is the irony of ensuring that you have the right talent driving your talent acquisition and development function. Think about the criticality of hiring decisions and make sure that you have invested adequately in the talent doing talent acquisition. Remember that many HR professionals despise the recruiting function. Do not overlook the importance of evaluating your hiring team to ensure that your organization is firing on all cylinders to make your talent acquisition strategy hum. I believe your most devoted, persistent, and talented people should be heading up your talent acquisition function.

Pro Tips (Not from Me)

Speaking of top-notch talent acquisition pros, many have influenced and blessed my career. Allow me to showcase a few and their perspectives on the characteristics you need on your team to truly attract and retain great talent.

Brad Owens, a talent enthusiast with years of recruiting under his belt, is practical, straightforward, thought-provoking, wickedly smart, and a tremendous problem-solver. We initially met after Brad dropped the mic (figuratively) on his DisruptHR pitch, "Why Your Applicants Hate You." Brad sees human resources' purpose to be "the best possible consultant for the employees, leaders, and business. If HR puts a consulting spin on what they're doing, they can change the trajectory of a business." With that context, you will gain a greater appreciation for Brad as he bristles at the thought that, too often, HR professionals are negatively associated with Toby from the hit NBC sitcom *The Office*.

In our conversation, he delved into why an HR professional's taskmaster strengths often serve them poorly in talent acquisition and development activities. Instead of discussing what a manager needs to achieve with the new hire, Brad explained that this critical hiring need is often seen as a task to be accomplished rather than viewed with a consultative approach from the very beginning. Brad believes that "HR must advance beyond order-taker and strive to be consultative." In his view, a consultant asks the right questions, listens, and can fill positions with individuals who serve the manager's needs . . . both explicit and implicit!

In other words, great HR recruiters get everyone involved in the recruiting process and seek feedback from *everyone*. You see the alignment in Brad's thinking even though he's using a different word . . . his "consultant" is our "boss."

Ask a million questions to get everything you need to know about what the manager needs and wants. Since there is no room for one million—said with a funny Mike Myers twang and pinky finger at the corner of your mouth—questions, here are a few to consider, starting with Brad's favorite:

» Can you tell me more about that?
» What does success look like to you?
» What is your biggest accomplishment and why does it make you proud?
» What impact did the last book you read have on you?
» How do you manage change?
» What type of work environment and culture do you work best in?
» What excites you the most about the work you are doing?
» How do you handle rejection or an objection to one of your ideas?
» Which company's purpose did you align to the most?

What good is it if you ask a killer question but do not take a sincere interest in the candidate's or hiring manager's perspective? Dave Ames, a talent acquisition executive from Columbus, Ohio, stressed that a recruiter should have "unbelievable listening skills if they're going to be able to capitalize on asking great questions and exploring." Having gone to high school together, I am proud of Dave's philosophy as he has grown up to be a world-class HR leader.

The perspective of my wise-beyond-her-years friend and talent acquisition pro Claire Stroh pulls together the earlier points made by Brad and Dave. Claire resides in Buffalo, NY, and we connected through our passion for organizing DisruptHR events. She "understands the power of a social network" and leads talent acquisition for an IT firm headquartered in downtown Buffalo. On top of that, she runs her own business that helps LinkedIn'ers effectively connect, post, and engage. Claire would sum up the points made by Brad and Dave about asking great questions and listening by encouraging HR and TA pros to be inquisitive.

I hope having a plan, being consultative, asking great questions, listening with intention, and being inquisitive helps you avoid the classic trap of unrealistic requirements. Hiring managers who fall into this notorious tendency put specific and often technical skills and knowledge at the top of their hiring criteria wish list. Do not get me wrong, it is important to hire competent people who know what they are doing. But could you imagine conducting a search where everyone is capable and has the appropriate skills so you can concentrate on hiring the right person and cultural fit for your organization?

There is a reason that the saying "hire for skill, fire for fit" exists.

As the department responsible for and at times complicit in hiring managers making mistake after mistake, it is paramount that HR builds the right talent team to springboard the hiring for the rest of your organization.

As we round out this all-important section on talent, let's take a mental break and think about the top talent at your company. While navigating the proper channels and playing the appropriate politics, consider discussing with a few of your top performers how joining the talent acquisition team may help to accelerate both the company's successes and their careers. Ask them to focus their skills on finding and maturing the best talent for your organization.

Once positioned in the right way, thoroughly share what a talent acquisition role is all about. As you discuss the responsibilities of your talent acquisition team, you just might be surprised to see their interest in being responsible for identifying new talent and growing the existing talent in your organization. Tell me a better role than being accountable for talent acquisition within any company that makes a difference in the business while getting to know *everyone* who works at the company.

Building a great talent acquisition team is critical to the success of your business. A key aspect that all great talent acquisition teams have as a part of their sourcing and TA strategy is a well-thought-out employee referral program. One of the most obvious opportunities to profoundly impact hiring the right talent within our firm is strategizing, planning, implementing, and maintaining an employee referral program. Why do we struggle to leverage our number one asset, our people, when attracting talent into our company? It's okay to say it: recruiters are salespeople. However, many aren't asking for referrals. Most people will give a referral if only they're asked to provide one!

To be more specific to the HR world, I am reminded of a recent discussion with Lou Adler, founder of The Adler Group known for its Win-Win Hiring programs using his Performance-Based Hiring[SM] system for finding and hiring exceptional talent. He suggested that the main key performance indicator (KPI) for successful recruiters is asking for and getting two referrals from every candidate you speak with.[1]

I am sure that Lou would encourage developing and promoting an employee referral program. It will take a little bit of coordination with your marketing, compensation, and finance teams to determine the exact dollar amount and timing your company is willing to pay an employee who refers a candidate who gets hired. I typically see compensation for employee referral programs ranging from $200 to $2,000 and being paid around ninety days after employment of the new hire who was referred by another employee. This is the easy part, while the most significant challenge seems to be asking employees for referrals and keeping the program front-and-center in your company. My suggestion for consistently branding your employee referral program is to recognize the referring and referred employees throughout your internal company communications. We printed a large, Styrofoam check with a dry eraser–friendly cover to promote Willory's employee referral program. We snapped a picture with the referring employee to remind the rest of our crew that our staffing team is open for referrals.

1. Lou Adler, "Here Are the Best (and Worst) Predictors of Quality of Hire," LinkedIn, *Talent Blog*, January 11, 2018, https://www.linkedin.com/business/talent/blog/talent-analytics/most-important-predictors-of-quality-of-hire.

Employee referral programs can be 70 to 90 percent less expensive than a search fee you might pay to a firm like Willory, and they increase the chances of your employees developing a best friend at work, which is a key indicator for employee engagement. It sounds like the opposite of Peter Tomarken's *double whammy* cry on the 1980s hit game show *Press Your Luck*!

If you are scratching your head and saying to yourself, "I am in talent acquisition or have these responsibilities and I don't want to add others to the team," I would challenge you to take a different perspective and realize that talent acquisition is about marketing and branding. Building your company's employer brand should be well thought out and carefully orchestrated. Consider the tone of your job descriptions, rejection letters, interview process, hiring managers, offer letters, and onboarding. Every aspect of your employer brand affects applicants, candidates, customers, vendors, and employees. Therefore, candidates and the community will notice when your company's most talented people who are genuinely interested in growing your company are sharing your organization's story with the world and making that lasting first impression.

As we consider that all of us are marketers in some form or fashion, especially those who have devoted their careers to talent acquisition and development, I often think of Pat Tourigny's success in transforming HR functions over the course of her career. Pat has held several highly influential roles such as head of talent acquisition at ING and senior vice president at Magellan Health. Now, she is a purpose-driven HR consultant and pours her heart into her volunteer work as a career coach to women in transition. Pat recently shared the idea that she could see "talent acquisition reporting into the marketing function." Pat saw the need for transformation by watching unemployment numbers shift, monitoring various talent acquisition metrics, and listening to hiring managers. Taking cues from marketing teams, the vision became more evident. She explained that the "future of talent acquisition lies in creating a value center that deploys the best of what successful marketing and brand teams do." According to Pat, recruiters should have skills as market-ers, digital citizens, design thinkers, data-based decision-makers, and career coaches. Engaging with external talent needs to shift from finding someone to fill a requisition (short-term and task-based) to casting a wide net to keep current on who and where the best talent in their industry is (long-term and strategic). And, instead of using traditional applicant tracking system (ATS), the new recruiter will master customer relationship management (CRM) technology like their marketing colleagues and connect with talent in new and more enduring ways.

By shifting how talent acquisition thinks of the work and subse-quent skills needed to acquire talent, Pat believes recruiters should, and will, become an extension of marketing and branding teams and support businesses as they grow. She is doing *HR Like a Marketer and a Boss*. "Talent attracts talent. Let the world know with your best people and a clear message how great your company is and build simple and repeatable processes and systems to tell that story as often and as effectively as you can. As a potentially overly complex aspect of your business and HR department, consider making talent acquisition as simple as that," explained Pat.

Enough said!

Chapter 10
Coach Managers

HR can't be everywhere. It's not in the best interest for your employees to feel that HR, the department often perceived as "Big Brother," is everywhere watching over their every move. Employees rarely quit a job or a company, but instead leave because of their manager or boss. So while you shouldn't be everywhere, you should also be active, aware, and available.

According to Development Dimensions International's (DDI) Frontline Leader Project completed in December 2019, more than half (57 percent) of employees leave a job because of their manager. To understand why this happens, the study revealed that the average age that an employee received their first management promotion was 36 years old.[1]

At the same time, it typically took four years before newly minted managers received training. Four years! The study calls this gap the "sink or swim" stage. Sadly, with every manager that sinks, an organization loses great people.

Additionally, the study shows that only one third of managers are female, and that no clear performance or educational component contributes to that significant disparity. The study also highlights the

---

1. Development Dimensions International, *The Frontline Leader Project: Exploring the Most Critical Segment of Leaders*, DDI, 2019, https://media.ddiworld.com/ebooks/FLL-eBook-interactive.pdf.

top sources of stress for managers, with the most common being "not enough time to do everything" and "office politics." Senior leaders suggest that the main weakness of managers is their lack of ability to handle conflict. One of the missing tool sets for these managers was training for "crucial conversations" and coaching skills. Managers left to sink or swim simply lack the ability to engage and motivate their teams.[2]

The final point from the study that is important to this discussion is a major indictment on HR. The study reveals that 90 percent of HR professionals believe that their company has a clearly defined mission. In comparison, only 28 percent of managers say that they, themselves, have a mission. This speaks loudly to the need for organizational buy-in to your purpose and core values and the repetition of it over and over and over again. Far too many managers and their employees are lost and rudderless.

Do you see the problem here? The challenge for HR is that countless employees are quitting their jobs because of their manager. Managers, who are too often promoted with little to no formal training on management basics, may feel overwhelmed by their role and are unable to effectively manage their time while lacking clear alignment between the company's purpose and their own.

To get additional perspective on this study, I asked for Tacy Byham's view. She has her PhD and is the CEO at DDI after taking over in 2015. Tacy has leveraged her role to create DDI's executive development practice and award-winning frontline leader development programs. She also pioneered DDI's focus on women in leadership with her "#LeadLikeAGirl" campaign. On top of that, Tacy also coauthored a book with Richard Wellins called *Your First Leadership Job: How Catalyst Leaders Bring Out the Best in Others*, which has sold over one hundred thousand copies.[3]

---

2. Development Dimensions International, *The Frontline Leader Project.*
3. Tacy Byham and Richard Wellins, *Your First Leadership Job: How Catalyst Leaders Bring Out the Best in Others*, Hoboken, NJ: Wiley, 2015.

As a second-generation CEO at DDI, Tacy credits her dad, Bill Byham, PhD, for much of her success. She is quick to point out that he started DDI in the basement of the Byham home in 1970, and the business has grown to have clients in ninety-three countries today. Bill Byham pioneered countless innovations in the HR space, including the following:

» The assessment center method,
» Behavior-based interviewing,
» The use of behavior modeling in supervisor and management training,
» Behavioral job analysis methodology as the basis for selection and training programs, and
» Acceleration pools to select and rapidly develop managers for high-level leadership positions.

Tacy's pedigree, hard work, and clear vision are the cornerstones for making a difference in the business community around the globe.

Tacy shared, "I am so proud to be a second-generation CEO for DDI while continuing the work that my father started nearly fifty years ago. At DDI, we transformed the workplace by introducing the assessment center methodology to the business world. Observing, evaluating, and predicting leadership behavior is now possible using a validated scientific approach."

My mind was blown to learn that Tacy's father invented the world's first behavior-based interviewing system, Targeted Selection®. Tacy said that "3,200 hiring decisions are made every hour using Targeted Selection®, and well over 20 million candidates have been successfully screened." So yes, if you have ever asked the question, "Tell me about a time when . . ." or collected STARs, you now know where that came from—DDI.

That level of expertise gives even more weight to DDI's leadership studies. Tacy shared, "The Frontline Leadership Project is significant in its findings that leaders are in a tough position as the bar for success keeps getting higher and higher. This group of leaders is responsible for so many critical functions, from attracting and retaining talent to fostering innovation and driving the adoption of digital technologies. But while expectations of frontline leaders are rising, they aren't getting the coaching, training, and support they need to be successful."

If your company currently lacks a leadership development plan or you believe your existing model needs a shot in the arm, take a look at the data from the DDI report. Then seek insights from someone like Tacy to build a plan to improve your leadership training and coaching process. This will help you justify the importance of making the investment in management training to your executive team.

Managers are often ill-prepared and therefore too overwhelmed to lead their employees effectively, and on top of that, the position lacks gender diversity. As a result, employees are disengaged at work. They quit because of their underskilled manager or the lack of a connection between their role and how it impacts company results and makes a difference in the community. Ultimately, they lack trust in and are not aligned to the company's purpose.

Don't Just Coach . . . Transform

The task may seem daunting, but it is fairly straightforward. Here are the *HR Like a Boss* suggestions to transform the way your company does business through effective management and leadership:

1. More thoroughly vet your manager candidates and get your high potentials thinking about leadership before a role becomes available.
2. Incorporate your diversity, equity, inclusion, and belonging (DEIB) strategy into the selection process to ensure a diverse set of managerial candidates.

3. Develop a plan to train your leaders on Day 1 (not Day 1,460).
4. Extend the leadership training from Day 1 to retirement for your managers, including the ongoing training, support, tools, resources, and coaching they need to succeed.
5. Make sure *everyone* understands the purpose and values of your company, and hire and fire based on these principles.

Let's break down these five critical steps outlined above in developing a successful group of leaders at your company.

The first point contends with the talent pool you have for managers. We previously mentioned the downfalls of the Peter Principle, wherein someone is promoted to a position they are ill-equipped to serve. Having a diverse set of managerial candidates is a critical first step in setting up your new managers, and ultimately your company, for success. A disciplined and structured succession planning process will help you identify your leadership gaps. As an outcome, a solid pipeline of managerial and leadership candidates should emerge from the exercise.

Once that pipeline is developed, build a simple vetting, information sharing, and educational process for your high potential or people manager standouts. Having a direct conversation with those that have expressed interest in or shown potential for a career in management will initially qualify your candidate pool. Then, a standard process could include showing the interested future leader a Management 101 training video along with an applicable book or e-book. This could be followed by a conversation with a recently promoted manager to discuss a "day-in-the-life" of a leader. It is of utmost importance to shoot it straight with each candidate, so they know the pros and cons of management at your company.

In a world where predominantly white male leaders crowd the leadership ranks, we need to lead by example and create diverse candidates for our leadership team. Taking a different approach by including unorthodox and disruptive thinkers to your leadership team, especially those with diverse backgrounds, untraditional career paths, or uncommon professional pedigrees, will lead to much broader perspectives, ways of doing business, and connections with your employees and community.

Too often, people seek out people who look, talk, and act like they do. I've made a conscious effort to improve my awareness, be mindful of my unconscious bias, learn from those different from me, and have an open mind. How? I've expanded my personal and professional network to include a wide array of people with varying sexual orientations, religious beliefs, nationalities, races, and political viewpoints. What I look for in the people I surround myself with are those who have an open and caring heart, a passion for what they do, an interest in making a difference, a command of their emotions, and an innate curiosity to learn from each other. Consider the impact that racial profiling following 9/11 had on people, culture, and our society. Narrow-minded thinking was exposed, and the importance of compassion for all people, not just those like you, grew in importance. We have a long way to go to reach perfection regarding diversity, equity, inclusion, and belonging (DEIB). In the meantime, we all must strive to provide and create equal opportunities, compensate equitably, and be intentional toward all walks of life at work and home.

If you do not have a DEIB plan or strategy, hire a professional consultant or DEIB consulting firm to help your team plan and implement strategies to make the necessary changes. Considering another opportunity for improvement, one of the most staggering points made in the DDI study was the four-year sink or swim time frame that new managers had between earning their first management job and receiving management training. Imagine the number of bad habits, mistakes, and poor decisions that could have been avoided with proper training and coaching. More importantly, think about the number of good employees you have lost—countless employees quit because of a bad boss. Handing out management jobs is the easy part, but coaching and developing managers to become leaders and executives is another level. Remember the old proverb, "Give a man a fish, and you'll feed him for a day. Teach a man to fish, and you've fed him for a lifetime." In this analogy, giving the new manager a leadership role is like giving them one fish. Teaching them how to fish in this analogy is HR's duty of enrolling the new manager in a structured and defined leadership development program that helps new managers, and existing leaders for that matter, develop skills for hiring, coaching, accountability, inspiration, and development.

Developing an effective leadership development program requires extensive research to create a plan that works for your company. You, of course, must have buy-in from your CEO and other executives. All great leaders have a coach, even beyond internal coaching. In the world of HR, there are endless mentors available to help. Many of the best HR teachers are well-connected in the HR community. Not to mention, I am willing to bet some fantastic leadership development coaches in your region can help you, your executive team, and all your employees reach new heights. Typically, these coaches will build programs that include the following:

» Detailed list of leadership competencies,
» A 360-degree assessment and review of the results,
» Discovery exploration with the managers, and
» Alignment meeting.

During this process, the new manager and their direct supervisor develop a customized leadership development plan that the manager owns. Then, they establish recurring meetings to ensure buy-in and progress of the plan coupled with quarterly leadership training on topics useful to the collective leadership team.

Willory hired Kathy Sullivan, an organizational development consultant, board-certified executive coach, and owner of Talent Principles, to orchestrate the leadership development planning and execution while providing executive coaching to our leadership team. With over twenty-five years of experience in human resources, talent development, and management consulting, she understands how critical it is to have effective leaders drive results for the business. Kathy said, "HR professionals have a unique perspective and can add increased value by learning more about how the business operates and understand what drives revenue and profitability. They often have visibility into the high-level business objectives and what is important to the executive leadership team and insight into the challenges and concerns of employees. This creates an opportunity to leverage systems and help close potential gaps in performance.

"When creating any leadership development program, it must be more than just developing key leadership competencies in leaders. It is imperative to help them understand how and when to apply those competencies within their context. This requires an understanding of the culture and strong critical thinking and decision-making skills. Working with an outside coach allows leaders to obtain an objective point of view and navigate various leadership challenges with the necessary support to overcome obstacles and drive accountability in achieving their developmental goals. This is often done in conjunction with their direct leader to align and support broader business objectives. Alignment and communication are key and can be further facilitated by the HR department."

Why has Kathy poured her heart and soul into cultivating leaders? She has seen the impact of effective and ineffective leadership within organizations throughout her career. Over the years, she has spent an increasing amount of time working with female leaders. As it turns out, many of Kathy's clients are working moms, including four of the directors on Willory's leadership team at the time this was written. She is coaching and holistically supporting them by helping them integrate and prioritize responsibilities while connecting them to their purpose. As a result of this theme in her work, Kathy is embarking on her own purpose-filled journey by penning a book called *Moms Eat First*. Kathy explained, "Part of what makes moms so special is the support and help they provide to everyone around them. Sometimes, it's at the expense of their well-being and can create burnout. Helping moms to identify their purpose and value, even apart from their work and family responsibilities, can help empower and motivate them to do things they may have previously felt were too risky to do. This is even more important as we see a growing number of parents working from home and managing kids, school, relationships, and life. Many moms bear the brunt of these unique and personally specific responsibilities and are choosing to leave the workforce as a result."

There is no doubt that someone doing *HR Like a Boss* helps to bridge this gap through the policies, programs, and benefits being offered, and views this as an opportunity to make a difference in their employees' lives.

Remember our earlier reference to Amy Powers from Chart Industries and their dedicated people plans? Like Amy and her team's work, it is up to HR to ensure that your leaders have the tools and resources to promote and ensure success. With Kathy's comments in mind and after seeing the impact of effective leadership on your employees, company, and society, you'll find that HR is perfectly positioned and key for ensuring that your managers have the tool kit for success.

At Willory, our leadership team collaborates with their dedicated coach through individual sessions. An important note to draw attention to is that the leadership team handles their own development plans. Our leaders are driving these discussions and managing their own leadership development. By taking this approach, we can ensure buy-in and alignment, as growing into an executive leader is multifaceted and can be trying and difficult at times. Yes, Willory has provided the forum for our leadership team to achieve this growth, but the leaders must be steering their own leadership development wheel.

A clear and straightforward leadership development plan is coupled with a firmwide scorecard to help our leaders and individual contributors achieve their core metrics. Individual development areas are addressed, core values are measured, and the firm's purpose achieves buy-in. We monitor daily and weekly activities with a monthly firmwide progress report and individual one-on-one meetings with employees and managers.

With the right balance and exchange of information between your employees and managers, who are appropriately trained and maintaining an ongoing accountability and development plan, you have an excellent foundation for an effective management team.

Consider a few unique points to strive for while directly developing relationships with your managers. First, ensure that the development plans your managers have in place for their employees are uniform in their format but unique to each individual. Using another sports analogy, expecting a role player to be a superstar is a quick way to lose and create frustration. Not everyone will be the number one sales performer or most productive employee in a particular department. Align the development plans to the skills and capabilities of each employee with an appropriate stretch potential for growth.

It's critical to ensure that your managers provide an environment in which their direct reports, your company's employees, have the opportunity to be themselves and do their best possible work. Understanding each employee's role within your company and harmonizing their personal and professional aspirations is vital to a successful manager and employee relationship. Some people simply want to do their job well, collect a paycheck, build their nest egg, be rewarded with meaningful work, and not be pressured into a promotion or advancing their career in a traditional sense. It is up to HR to ensure that everyone understands and respects each other and their role and provides an appropriate balance amongst your team.

Nobody's Perfect

As the business community is not a utopia, we can't lose sight of the pure and simple fact that employees will turn over. Some are not a good fit, and some underperform. Facing these challenges is part of the gig for HR pros. Poorly performing team members and employees can drain the spirit of your team, producing an accompanying negative impact on your good employees and their productivity. As I am sure you have experienced, a lot of time is spent on employees who are struggling and performing below expectations. HR and managers devote an unbalanced amount of time working through strategies to improve, disciplinary meetings, feedback sessions, and performance improvement plans. After all, the squeaky wheel gets the grease.

I've sadly lost a ton of time and firm productivity to underperforming employees. In no way am I saying don't spend time trying to help a struggling employee. Instead, set a structured time frame and establish the milestones that will prompt the next steps to coach them up or out of your firm. This is the unpleasant truth of doing business and managing your human resources effectively.

We can't end this portion on coaching managers and leaders on that note, but we can encourage you to reconcile what we discussed in this section and compare it to the leadership development plan that you have in place at your company. With HR's responsibility within an organization, you should always be asking every employee, manager, and executive, "What do you need from me to be successful in your role?" and "How are you developing to reach your personal and professional aspirations?" A key point in getting managers to perform at a high level is alignment to the desired results of your employees, business, and community. Get your managers aligned to what their people need while doing what it takes to help the organization. In HR, it is up to you to model this behavior and demand that everyone is on the same page (even if they disagree). This behavior will ensure that your managers follow your lead in developing each employee in your company.

Create Clarity

I started this section with a straightforward and clear message: as an HR professional, it is *your* responsibility to create clarity in your organization. In companies of every size, we see employees, entire departments, and often the whole company unable to answer important questions, like, "What is our plan to achieve our vision and purpose?" "What do you expect from your employees to achieve that plan?" and "What should be done to meet them where they are at?" Someone doing *HR Like a Boss* knows their organization better than anyone else and can identify what makes it unique and make it crystal clear for their employees, customers, partners, and so on.

As we begin this journey of creating clarity within your organization, take a moment to grab a bowl or sugar cone full of your favorite ice cream. Nothing clears my mind more and brings me pure joy than the delicious taste of ice cream. Maybe the simplicity of the experience or the reminders of childhood joy came with that unique combination of ice, cream, and sugar.

On top of that, Zoe Switzer, CHRO from Columbus, Ohio, with varied experience, including a sweet one at Jeni's Splendid Ice Creams, shared a simple anecdote with me on the subject of clarity. She suggested that whenever *anything* comes into her HR department, the primary responsibility of her team is to ensure that it leaves with more clarity while minimizing any drama associated with the people, events, or experience.

Zoe's approach seems almost too simple. However, some would argue that simplicity is the main ingredient when making the delicious treat of clarity.

Okay, I hope you enjoyed your ice cream social. That is enough sweet talk; now back to doing *HR Like a Boss.*

How does Zoe do it? It starts with talking to people and truly listening to their concerns. By stopping what you are doing, turning off your phone, and taking an "I am all in" on this discussion approach, you increase your ability to connect with people and understand what is truly going on. Let's stop here to shine the light on what now seems like the forgotten art and skill of listening.

When employees are confused or frustrated at work, something is typically missing or off. You will see a disconnect between what is expected and what is happening. This is the result of a lack of understanding or confusion about what should be done by who and how often. This lack of clarity causes a ripple effect on employee relationships, job performance, department unity, and company outcomes. There is no better function within an organization than the HR team to build a path to clarity.

In doing so, there's a transition we need to make as professionals as we increasingly collaborate with others as our organization grows. When I think back to when I started Willory, I was a solo act, a band of one. To keep with our theme of eighties rock giants, I was much like Prince on his early albums. I played all the instruments myself, so I didn't need to give precise instructions or directions to anyone else—I didn't need to write or speak clearly about where the organization was headed. Still, I just needed to keep the thoughts straight in my head. As Prince's popularity grew, he hired a band, The Revolution, and proceeded to experience the heyday of his career because he had grown into a musician who could collaborate with others, bringing the most out of his colleagues (bandmates).

For the record, I do believe this is the first time I or anyone else has ever compared me to Prince. Anyway, as my firm grew and I started to hire employees, it was critical to communicate my vision, train my new employees, and get everyone working effectively.

Doing *HR Like a Boss* includes communicating purpose, values, and vision with precision and transparency on where the organization is going, why it is going there, and how we are going to get there. When combined with implicit and simple tasks that need to be done by departments and the individuals within those functions, the complex, often tangled, and possibly winding nature of the business can become as clear as Whitney Houston's performance of "The Star-Spangled Banner" at the 1991 Super Bowl. When employees are aligned with the purpose of the business and vice versa, your company will sing. It's HR's responsibility to get all departments aligned with the CEO and their vision for the business to see where the company is going and how to get there.

In my own life, creating clarity has been the most challenging aspect of my professional development, especially as the span of my control widened. Being clear and concise was not a natural-born instinct of mine, and it has not come easily for me. In my professional career, I work diligently to clarify what we're trying to do, why, and how we're trying to do it, all while ensuring everyone on our team is on the same page. I began to improve my ability to create clarity when I was more authentic and vulnerable with my team by sharing with them what I was thinking about the challenges and opportunities that we faced as a business. By communicating my thoughts and insights with those on my team, I would go through an iterative process by asking questions of and getting insights from them. For example, we have evolved to repeat our purpose, core values, and goals monthly. By doing so, we ensure alignment to purpose and core values while ensuring we remain on track to reach our goals.

HR has a unique opportunity to make sure that specific goals, projects, and so on align with what the business is trying to achieve. If you let people in your business pigeonhole you as a tactical hiring and payroll engine, you're *not* doing *HR Like a Boss* and the coveted seat at the table will elude you.

One person immediately comes to mind when I think of *clear is kind* communication: George Sample. George has a profound ability to be short, direct, and concise with his communication. As I develop my own skills for clarity and conciseness, I find myself marveling at how he speaks so succinctly.

We highlighted George's prowess previously, but his direct and clear communication delivers results. Do not get me wrong; George is not short. He is over six feet and a former college football standout. There it is, another bad dad joke.

To get back to the point, George is always eloquent and clear with his two to three sentence answers that are rich beyond words and precise to keep everyone's attention. George has used his communication skills to rise in the ranks in his previous roles while giving back to the HR field in his Society for Human Resource Management (SHRM) leadership capacity.

To be more like George with your communication, you must clarify what's going on within your purview by creating clarity in the most important activities at your company. The best way to be clear and concise is through preparedness, alignment, and practice. The larger the organization, the harder it will be to have global reach, but in HR, you're in the right department to make a difference.

Doing *HR Like a Boss* means stepping in and leading the CEO through the process to put together a clear company purpose and core values leading into your strategic plan. If you serve in HR in an organization with a CEO that is not, for whatever reason, good at creating clarity, setting a vision, and developing core capabilities, then creating corporate clarity falls on you or someone on your HR team.

As for the company's purpose and core values, I strongly recommend that you take a collaborative approach across your entire company. Here are the steps:

1. Create a specific definition of the company's purpose and core values.
   a. Purpose is the reason your company exists in the first place; it should be aspirational and four words or less.
   b. What are the core items that you want every single employee to adhere to? Core values are your beliefs and standards by how you will achieve your goals. We typically see companies have three to seven core values that are led by action statements of one to four words each.
2. Poll your workforce about what they think your company's purpose and core values are.
3. Collect and analyze the results.
4. If your company is big, build a focus group to make the best suggestions and dissect the best few options. If your company has under a hundred employees, I suggest

involving everyone in this discussion. Remember, your purpose should be aspirational and four words or less, and your core values are your company's barometer and nonnegotiables.

Creating clarity goes beyond a checklist of corporate communications; it's also necessary to let employees know how their individual and specific roles are to help the business achieve its goals. It's HR's job to make sure that people are in place to deliver on the vision set forth for your business—and if they are not, to develop them or find ones that can help you achieve your goals.

Speaking of achievement, Michelle Leedy is one of the most engaging, likable, and dynamic HR executives that I know. She is an expert on delivering organizational clarity and knows the importance of getting everyone on the same page. On top of that, Michelle is active in the community while putting her family first in everything she does.

Michelle shared, "It's so important to make sure everything is clear and the best way to do so is to simplify everything down to an eighth-grade level. Not because employees cannot consume it otherwise, but it is just simpler and more straightforward."

She continued on to suggest, "When there is not a value add that is clear, there is lack of buy-in or investment from your employees. Your employees will begin to ask why they would invest in something not valuable. To them, it would feel like something they *have* to do. Even worse, sometimes employees might be in roles that they feel that they are not adding value to the company or more importantly the purpose of the organization."

Michelle continued to share her wisdom by saying, "It is HR's responsibility to help everyone in an organization understand where they add value and how they align to the business." Despite great intentions, Michelle said, "HR can get caught up in its own acronyms and what they are doing and lose sight that HR is there to serve a greater calling, the employees and the business."

Michelle stressed that the human resources function "must be closely tethered to what the vision and purpose of the business is and how we can make that impact on the organization, your employees, and ultimately the community."

With Michelle's clear message in mind, I want to encourage you to close your eyes for a moment and imagine that your CEO, executive team, middle management, and employees are all abundantly clear about what your organization is trying to achieve. Envision a place where each employee and department understands their role in reaching a clearly set vision. Then, visualize HR's role in driving and maintaining a clear path to help your organization achieve its goals. Picture a workforce that is aligned and engaged while understanding how their role positively impacts the results the business is trying to achieve. Finally, end this visualization exercise by imagining a community that is so profoundly impacted by the resources provided by your company's success that you can see the positive difference in the surrounding neighborhoods, schools, and parks.

With the appropriate amount of care and concern for alignment and clarity, all of it is possible!

Chapter 11
Communicate Consistently

Before diving headfirst into communicating consistently, think about the best relationship you currently have. There is likely a foundation of transparency, mutual respect, two-way dialogue, reciprocal safety in the conversations, appreciation, and a level of love. Beyond the specifics of the relationship, how is the communication between the two of you?

Now, take a moment to reflect on the relationships that cause you the most stress. We all have people in our lives that will always be there, but with whom communication is . . . difficult. While positive relationships have transparency, safety, and a two-way dialogue based on mutual respect, troubling relationships are missing one or all three of these components of fruitful relationships.

Communication Is a Necessary Skill

As HR professionals, our impact is often measured by the *healthy* relationships we create and maintain. Don't be held back in your relationship-building endeavors because of (your) poor communication skills. Bad communication is way more than just being a poor communicator.

Inferior communication in HR can also mean no communication or inconsistent communication. HR has the unique opportunity to ensure consistent corporate communication that fills in the blanks for employees regarding what is happening. Without it, employees will tell themselves endless stories that are probably far worse than the truth which can cause mistrust, disengagement, and an overall decrease in productivity.

Communicating clearly and concisely is a necessary skill for the contemporary worker. For many, this skill isn't innate but is instead learned. It's your responsibility to the employees of your organization to communicate distinctly and directly—and to give them the resources to do so themselves.

Communicating in a practical, consistent basis is a differentiator for someone doing *HR Like a Boss*. It's so important that these recommendations should seem quite familiar from the sections on receiving and giving feedback.

It's your job to overcome both your own and your employees' poor communication practices that often stem from the following:

- » Emotionally charged individuals telling themselves detrimental stories;
- » Poor habits;
- » Laziness in pockets of your organization;
- » Failure to formulate thoughts before speaking;
- » Inability to be direct and concise, and meandering instead of getting to the point;
- » Inability to choose the right words, including the inability to listen to the words the other people are using;
- » Desire to talk versus a desire to communicate; and
- » Competitive natures resulting in a desire to be "right" versus getting it right.

Improving how you communicate isn't an overnight change, and there are many ways you can approach it. I am not writing a book on communication, but I do have some book recommendations, including Dale Carnegie's *How to Win Friends and Influence People*, Keith Ferrazzi and Tahl Raz's *Never Eat Alone*, Mark Goulston's *Just Listen*, and *Crucial Conversations*.

Doing *HR Like a Boss* means communicating effectively and consistently and helping employees in your organization do the same. Does your organization have leaders that are looked at as secretive and untrustworthy? Do you have a leader known for their screaming tirades or who takes too long to reach their point?

Through education and building agreed-upon frameworks, your organization can transcend many issues that stem from poor or no dialogue. It's possible to create a world where updates and changes are communicated consistently by managers, executives, and HR.

Perhaps sadly for the non-bosses, everything we do in HR is not about us! Rather, doing *HR Like a Boss* means impacting others, which includes helping others (employees) achieve their absolute best self in their professional journey. HR needs to demonstrate the power of consistent, clear, and concise communication and its impact on the people, departments, and organization.

No one has done this better and in her own way than Patti Stumpp, human resources leader of hypergrowth for-profit and well-respected nonprofit organizations. Patti provides a unique perspective, suggesting that to do *HR Like a Boss,* "you have to use business language, not HR language while exercising and speaking with authority." She went on to say, "if you are afraid to speak up, then you should not be in HR as speaking up is quite literally your job."

Know Your Audience

When it comes to communication and creating an impact, the single most important thing for someone doing *HR Like a Boss* is to know their audience.

Imagine you're presenting in Spanish to a group of employees who only speak French. It doesn't matter how much you prepare, how beautiful your presentation is, or how engaging you are; you simply won't understand each other . . . you won't connect. Yes, it's incredibly important to know what you want to say, but if you don't understand how to connect with your audience, you won't be able to develop a trusting, transparent, and safe two-way dialogue.

Now, the chances are that this scenario would never play out in the real world (although I'm surprised there isn't a *Seinfeld* episode about this), but at Willory, we've seen similar "foreign language" situations happen when implementing a new HR technology system. Vendors use jargon, acronyms, and crafted words with a specific meaning (to them), but clients don't always use those same words, nor do they understand the language a vendor is speaking. It's our consultants' job to understand both audiences and create a shared level of understanding. We need to understand the language a customer speaks rather than forcing them to adapt to us. This includes the "languages" that different departments within an organization speak. Some departments are tech-savvy; some aren't. Some speak your language, and some won't. How you prepare to train your marketing team on a new human capital management (HCM) system will be very different from how you train HR, different from finance, and so on.

As someone doing *HR Like a Boss*, take a moment to think about the following questions and considerations before approaching a conversation:

» Is your audience made up of different personality types? Extroverts may love sharing ideas, but introverts might be turned off if you force them to stand up and speak to the group.

» What generation are you speaking with? We know there are distinct differences between the generations, but understanding how you can use those differences in a workplace setting will set you apart from people who refuse to work through the differences.

» What is their expertise (or lack of) in the subject? If you're speaking to someone outside of HR about benefits models, you will have to approach the discussion in a very different way.

» What is the jargon related to the job used by this group? "Stat" to a medical doctor is going to mean something very different than it would to someone in an analytical field.

Knowing your audience—similar to minimizing distractions—is a respectful part of communication. It shows that you care about what you have to say and that you respect how your communication partner needs to receive the information. Doing so will help your organization save time and money and minimize misunderstandings.

Consistency Is Your Brand's Foundation

From a company perspective, communication—consistent or otherwise—directly reflects your company's brand. In the past, HR and marketing were typically not aligned. But in the last several years, I've seen the two functions improving relations and recognizing the value of working together. Willory's director of marketing, Bridgette Klein, often insists we review marketing trends because they're a relevant predictor of what the future of HR might look like.

Building a Brand Is Intentional

A brand is much more than what people think when they see your company logo; it includes the reputation your organization has with employees, the community, and outsiders, like candidates, vendors, partners, local government officials, and so on.

Dani Kimble, a marketing consultant from Wadsworth, OH, understands the relationship between marketing and HR. I met Dani through the local Society for Human Resource Management (SHRM) chapter and found her to drive culture by partnering and working tirelessly with her HR colleagues and employees at her company.

As a marketing professional, Dani sees the purpose of HR to be connecting people to the organization's key purpose and mission. HR, she said, "has the privilege to explain the 'why' behind the work people do and give it true meaning and purpose. When people feel fulfilled about the work they do, not only are they better performers, but that positivity bleeds into all areas of their lives."

New hires, resignations, retirements, acquisitions, unionization, and much more are all forces that will impact your company and, with it, evolve your culture and the accompanying brand. Through all of these inevitable changes, HR must be consistent with its communication. This includes the company's standards for itself, including its purpose, mission, vision, values, and culture. Of course, all of these will need to be reviewed and tweaked as things change, but the consistent delivery and reminder of what is most important should come from HR (with an assist from marketing).

As we mentioned before, Willory begins each firm-wide meeting with a commitment to the meeting, then a reminder and discussion about our purpose and our core values. It is an effort to reiterate our purpose and ensure we are all focused and rowing in the same direction. We discuss successes that we have achieved and where we fell short in living up to our goal. Our team also shares personal stories of living by the "Willory Way," our core values.

What about your company? Can employees in your company tell you what your company's purpose and core values are? It is less important to memorize them and recite them word-for-word than to be able to internalize their meaning and intent so they can be a reflective piece and contributor to your company's culture. If your employees aren't there (yet), collaborate with your HR colleagues, leadership, and marketing to ensure everyone is on the same page and build a model for consistent and clear communication.

There is no instant recipe or quick approach to create a strong culture and brand. It takes time to work with your marketing (or communications, public relations, or whatever your organization calls it) to build a brand and align it with your purpose, products, values, and people. Work to make sure you carefully construct your message around your organization's strategy and align your leadership to its tone, tenor, and goals. Only consistent communication can overcome daily distractions and inevitable organizational changes.

Make It Habitual

Consistent communication needs to be developed into a habit for those practicing *HR Like a Boss*. Consider the baggage you carry for some employees, mainly through no fault of your own; some are simply scared of (getting fired by) HR. Taking steps like consistently communicating or communicating with people at a consistent time takes away the edge of thinking, "Oh no, HR is in the room, there's only one reason for that . . . I'm being fired."

Instead, consistent communication sets the stage for employees to be more receptive and open to your messages. Why? Consistency can come in various forms, including responding to emails within twenty-four hours or responding to emails at a predictable, set time of day. Your habit of communicating regularly tempers anxiety and encourages dialogue. You should also be aware of your emotions and communicate in a measured, consistent manner. Avoid saying "we need to talk" without giving any details or specifics about the agenda.

Has this happened to you? Think back to the last time someone asked to "talk to you" without giving more details. Did you start to fret about the worst-case scenario? Far too often ambiguity worries people. Don't create this sort of situation.

Encourage your leadership team to deliver consistent summations to their teams via daily, weekly, and monthly communications. I recommend looking at a variety of delivery methods as they might reach out to different audiences. These methods can include team meetings, town halls, open office hours, email, company portal, and physical mail (especially great for expressing gratitude). No matter what you do, make sure there's a level of consistency. Abandoning one method for another every month is going to be disruptive to the organization.

One of my former colleagues at Willory, Philip Major, who wins the distinction of the best DisruptHR presentation I've seen, reminded me that "words really do matter." When doing *HR Like a Boss*, the words we use should be deliberate and chosen with care. Use words that have a single meaning and cannot be misinterpreted. If you're using terms that have the potential to be misunderstood or have multiple meanings, provide clarity with definitions. Pay attention to people's reactions, and if it doesn't seem like they understand, stop and take the time to address the confusion right away.

Listening Comes Before Talking

Unfortunately, creating a culture around communicating consistently doesn't end with knowing your audience, being diligent with your brand, or even showcasing good habits. In order to be different and embody what it means to do *HR Like a Boss*, you have to look at communication as the cornerstone of all that you do. This doesn't mean simply talking a lot; it means harnessing the power of two-way dialogue to listen and share in a way that allows both parties to receive the message and understand each other. One key factor in two-way dialogue is feedback. Great communicators are often the best listeners. Don't ignore this vital piece by steamrolling over people and not being receptive to it.

Let's get back to my friend and marketer Dani Kimble. When I spoke with Dani for the *HR Like a Boss* podcast, she shared how she sees standout HR professionals as empathetic listeners and suggested that "empathetic listening is listening to people without the intention of thinking about what your response is going to be. Actively listening to them shows them you care about them. I think if people in the workplace have an avenue or somebody that they can talk to that they know is truly listening to their needs and cares about them, there is so much value there."

It's an opportunity to (dare I repeat myself) be empathetic and do *HR Like a Boss*! My favorite tips for empathetic listening include the following:

1. Give people your undivided attention and show that you are listening carefully.
2. Be sure to create safety in your conversations.
3. Restate or repeat back as you talk. (Consider the concept of mirroring.)
4. Silence isn't the enemy, so don't be afraid of it and maybe even embrace it.
5. Sometimes what isn't said is just as important as what is said.
6. Be mindful of your own emotions and don't take things personally.

Similar to the other facets of consistent communication, empathetic listening isn't for everyone. However, it's imperative to the success of your organization that you and the HR professionals on your team are the best listeners possible. By listening properly, you are set up for success and prepared to communicate clearly and consistently.

Trust Your Gut

Trusting your gut sounds so cliché; I know. But, when done thoughtfully and with intention, it becomes a reliable differentiator for seasoned pros who do *HR Like a Boss*. The ability to combine the heady use of facts and data with an appropriate slice of gut instinct and intuition evolves through years of experiences, including both successes and failures. Effectively navigating through the gray and using your wisdom and experience can really be handy when dealing with an employee issue that circumvents a particular policy or when a strategic business decision must be made to mitigate a threat to your business.

When a situation is unclear or there are personal circumstances that cause you to make an unprecedented call, stand steadfast to your and your company's culture, core values, and purpose. Let's dissect stories, suggestions, and wisdom that allow you to be consistent when facing a tough decision that requires you to trust your gut.

HR professionals face a number of these situations on a daily, monthly, and yearly basis. Someone doing *HR Like a Boss* sees these scenarios as an opportunity to exemplify the characteristics of a consummate HR professional. Someone who weighs the pros and cons when making decisions will further the company's interests while advancing the individual employee's development.

All of this ties back to impacting your employees' lives, resulting in improved company production, attainment of your purpose, and positive impacts on the community. These decisions, big or small, earn your and your company's reputation with its employees and the community. Sometimes, this means you have to let someone go or help them find another opportunity. These situations also present an opportunity for you to create a new precedent based upon a circumstance which might include an employee's fight against cancer, the loss of a loved one, or an action taken that was best for the employee but maybe not for the company.

When encountering a situation that requires a delicate balance between policy and reality, I *always* start with purpose and values. These two pillars provide a guidepost to make really tough decisions that involve unique and peculiar circumstances.

Navigating the Gray

When dissecting a gray area and how to navigate it most effectively, I immediately turn to Steve Harris. Steve has advanced his HR executive career and entrepreneurial experience to bring a tremendously steady hand to his employers and network of clients, employees, and connections, all of whom are fortunate to know him. Steve uses the term "true north" when navigating unique and complex matters. He prides himself on contrarian thought and business-focused decision-making. When I met Steve, he was coming off a traditional HR career path with stints at Timken Company and National City Bank. I remember our very first encounter in 2010 at a local coffee shop. We were both feeling each other out as we had recently launched our businesses, with him growing an HR consultancy. Steve stood out to me as a client-focused, business-minded professional.

Today, he is driving results that are making a difference in his employees' lives and customers' businesses. When Steve recently joined the *HR Like a Boss* podcast, we talked about working in the gray, and he shared a few anecdotal tips that really stuck with me. Steve emphasized how "you must trust your gut when dealing in the gray areas. We would like to be able to measure everything and all decisions would be straightforward and easy. It would take HR (and all leaders for that matter) off the hook of making tough decisions."

Steve shared that he is a "sucker for really solid, fundamental leadership. It is up to a leader to effectively operate in gray areas. In those circumstances that it is more of a feel, leaders may be able to back into measurements to support how you really think about a situation. Effectively navigating gray areas is a necessity in HR and maybe more so leadership. By being consistent in your approach and facilitating open dialogue, HR professionals set up their employees and their organization for success. It takes courage and vulnerability to make difficult decisions and brave leaders stand out in this respect."

Continuing with the topic of dealing in the gray, Steve suggested that the next phase of making tough decisions involves getting input and perspective from others around or involved in the situation. He recommended that "after you have looked at the situation from the lens of your core values and purpose, it is important to take time to speak with others within the organization to gauge their opinion and perspective. It is amazing how quick we are to make decisions when a little dose of patience and perspective can more clearly define the path you should take. In doing so, it's been my experience that to truly understand the result that you are trying to achieve, you need to take the required time needed to dissect the issue in front of you and carefully consider your options. By taking time to collect information, gain perspective, and learn from others who have faced similar situations, you will be further manned with information to make the call."

Another example of an HR pro relying on his gut is Joe Szafraniec. I typically use the phrase "OG Boss" when describing Joe. I met Joe at the beginning of my professional career, and he stood out from others whom I worked with because of the immediate investment he made in our relationship and his keen focus on driving business results through his expertise in HR. He was doing *HR Like a Boss* well before the phrase was coined. As a matter of fact, my experience working with Joe initially set the bar for what it took to do amazingly awesome HR.

With that in mind, Joe always encourages a strong consideration of the moral and ethical components of the matter and the comfort of you and your company with applying these components to the situation you are navigating—and that should *live* in your gut. When making really tough decisions, you must look at the things that will keep you up at night staring at your ceiling, or in my case (because I have no issue falling asleep at night), cause you to wake up a couple of hours before your morning alarm is set to go off.

Digging into your moral principles and humanizing the decision provides an incredible amount of context and perspective to make the right choice. This can be more easily accomplished if your organization has a clearly defined set of ethics, core values, and principles. Often, you can reference your company's employee handbook (you developed it for a reason) and explore some of the foundational principles and policies that might provide some unbiased perspectives, as you and your organization drafted these organizational pillars for these "in the gray" moments.

Joe provided some wise input on this topic, and he showed his passion for this important component of doing *HR Like a Boss* in his following considerations:

> *I have found that new leaders can be initially surprised by "in the gray" moments and how often they arise. But with time and experience, leaders come to recognize these situations when they see them and that, among other things, these situations are fundamentally business challenges that can oftentimes be resolved by employing a few time-tested methods.*
>
> *Key to the success of these methods is a strong moral compass (on the part of both individuals and companies), coupled with a well-developed and clearly articulated set of core values and underlying principles, which guide the course of collective and individual conduct.*
>
> *With this moral compass serving to define the standard, the various elements of the "in the gray" issue can be tested against that standard. A particularly useful method I use for this process is a mix of "what if" questions, creating various scenarios and outwardly considering the impact different courses of action on a variety of constituents—the business, its employees, their families, and the communities in which they live.*
>
> *From there, I think about the truth I would have to tell— to these constituents and, even more personally, what truth I would have to tell my family and friends face-to-face, or*

the public-at-large on the nightly news or the front page of the newspaper.

Over the years, I have found that a reasoned and well-thought-out course of action can be achieved by asking these types of questions, then debating the pros and cons of how the approaches meet, exceed, or fall short of the standard.

In short, the key is having that ethical standard, acting with integrity and courage, and knowing yourself.

Embrace the Challenges

After taking an ethical viewpoint, let's go inside your head and into your gut, exposing your vulnerability to head down this path, whatever place it may take you, with courage and determination. Great leaders consider every challenge that requires a tough call to be an opportunity for you and the other person impacted by this decision. There is a reason the saying "everything happens for a reason" can be profound. You need to embrace challenging decisions and take responsibility very seriously. There's a good reason that someone trusted you to make difficult decisions. Don't get overwhelmed by circumstances and become stuck, unable to make a call for fear that you may make the wrong decision.

The weight of decision-making is often a self-inflicted burden. If you are waffling to make a decision and feel overwhelmed, consider two really important facts. The first is that you, yourself, did not do anything wrong and are an innocent bystander who most likely had nothing to do with the situation. You are simply tasked with helping those who are involved find a peaceful solution that remains consistent with how your company operates. Second, the decision you are about to make is rarely (if ever) fatal to the career of the person in question. In many situations, the employee ends up in a better place as a result of the tough decision that was made.

One final thing to remember when trusting your gut is to be vulnerable with those involved. The HR pros that I have seen navigate difficult situations and make even more challenging decisions are brutally honest about the circumstances, their perspective, and ultimately their expertise in the area in question. Sincerity and candor are two of the most valuable tools you can use when facing a difficult, unclear situation that requires delicacy from an HR perspective.

By being true to your purpose and values, examining the matter from an ethical viewpoint, taking the necessary time to consider all the factors, and approaching the responsibility that you face with vulnerability and courage, you are equipped to trust your gut and make those tough decisions. This experience gives you insights into how you, your leaders, and your employees react and respond to complicated matters, arming you with more of those *HR Like a Boss* superpowers!

Chapter 12
Build Relationships

B ased upon the nature of your role in human resources, do you feel the need to be guarded and at arm's length with your relationships at work? If so, how do you think this is impacting your ability to do amazingly awesome HR? I ask these questions as I reflect on the dichotomy that exists about what is deemed acceptable when it comes to workplace relationships.

On one hand, I remember being perplexed the first time that I took the Gallup Q12 engagement survey.[1] The question that took me aback the most was "Do you have a *best* friend at work?" Maybe taken aback is too strong of a phrase, but when I examined the question and looked at the results for our firm, it seemed the addition of the word *best* in the question changed the dynamic of the responses.

On the other hand, there are many people who feel that they leave their personal life and relationships at home and do not think it is appropriate to develop deep relationships at work.

The point of this chapter is neither. It is not about finding a best friend at work. That seems unrealistic. A best friend is a singular relationship that stands above all others, and the idea that people

1. The Gallup® Q12® survey questions are Gallup proprietary information and are protected by law. You may not administer a survey with any of the Q12® survey questions or reproduce them without written consent from Gallup. Copyright 1993–1998 Gallup, Inc. Gallup® and Q12® are trademarks of Gallup, Inc. All rights reserved.

will develop that kind of friendship at work seems to be a stretch. Contrary to that, it seems off-putting and a missed opportunity to shut down the idea that you can develop meaningful and important relationships at work.

Like many things in life, striking the right balance with relationships at work is somewhere in the middle of these two schools of thought. By being intentional about forming bonds with colleagues, team members, and associates, you increase your chances of enjoying the work that you do and spending it with people that you like. One of the great joys that I have heard time and again from people who have retired from the workforce is that they enjoy not having to deal with the stresses of work but really miss the people.

If you are looking to do *HR Like a Boss,* it is HR's responsibility to connect the people to the business and make an impact on employees, the company, and the community. We must carefully examine the societal factors like relationships at work that can positively influence employees' experience and their level of engagement at work. There is a balance that exists that ensures employees are being effective at doing their jobs while fostering an environment to build lifelong relationships that have a robust number of intrinsic benefits that can change the lives of someone in a meaningful and beautiful way.

Why must we do this? Countless studies have indicated that the majority of employees do not feel engaged at work, and they believe that their employers do not care about them in a meaningful way. It seems borderline cruel to allow that type of sentiment to continue under the strenuous relationship that can exist between employee and employer. I have to believe that this turns the stomach of someone aspiring to do *HR Like a Boss.* We need to figure out a different way, a better way, to engage our employees and align the goals of our organization with the workforce. When done right, the results affect our people, company, and community in a profoundly positive way.

Building relationships at work leads to increased productivity, improved employee engagement, and potentially life-changing personal impact. These are all excellent reasons to step up your building-lasting-relationships-at-work game. Here is how you do it.

Before getting into the specifics, let me express this public service announcement on building relationships. I have been told on countless occasions by HR pros that they love having specific steps to do things, especially from authors in books. Please note that I am not a relationship-building expert like Dr. Ruth or Dear Abby. However, I feel compelled to share that professionalism is undoubtedly required in building respectful and appropriate work-place relationships in a caring and reliable way while not stepping across the line in a sexual, fraternal, demonizing, or whimsical manner. Don't get distracted from the reason you are there—to get a job done. The simple guidepost here is to ALWAYS keep things appropriate.

How to Build *HR Like a Boss* Relationships

Let's dive into the steps according to the author of this book (which is my only qualification other than over twenty-five-plus years of building personal relationships at work).

First, don't think you have to be friends with everyone. Yes, you should be friendly to everyone, but building long-lasting rela-tionships depends on the two people who make the best connec-tion. Plus, it takes an investment of time to truly foster meaningful friendships. As I have grown older, my relationships have become fewer but deeper compared to when I was friends with a hundred people during my high school days. Being selective and authentic to who you are is an important first step toward forming meaning-ful friendships.

Once you have identified a relationship that is worth fostering, begin to make a mutually agreeable effort. Now, I use the term mutually agreeable in loose terms as we are not looking to get this in writing or making a verbal contract (although if that is your thing, be my guest). What I am suggesting is leaning into the relationship by going to lunch, sharing a cup of coffee, getting your families together, or heading to Top Golf for an afternoon of fun. In doing so, see if your new friends mutually reciprocate by asking you to get together to break bread, chat over a cup of joe, or take a walk together with your kids. If, for some reason, you are the only one making this effort or vice versa, take stock of the meaning of this one-way relationship and lean in if you so choose or address the *elephant in the room* by simply stating that you enjoy your new friend's company and wonder if the feeling is mutual.

I realize that this may seem a bit forward, but I am not interested in wasting my time on a relationship that feels one-sided. I have been burned in the past and invested a ton of my time and effort only to find that the other person was not into the relationship the same way. Yes, it hurt for a bit, but I was so glad to know so that I could pour my heart and soul into the relationships that had an appropriate give-and-take.

I work really hard to be diligent in my efforts as people can get very lazy with their relationships. They become complacent and do not put in the necessary energy to express their admiration for others through things like kindness and acts of service and, as a result, the relationships can erode or begin to become toxic.

One of the best ways to avoid complacency in a relationship is to take a sincere interest in your friend's important interests. Be curious, ask questions, and take the time to learn about whatever it might be. I have learned a ton about watercolor paintings, remote control cars, ordained ministry, fantasy football, real estate investing, Harry Potter, gymnastics, boating, 1980s pop culture, Peloton bikes, cryptocurrency, and the list could go on and on. Nothing feels better than when someone takes an interest in you and what you do and they express a genuine enthusiasm in learning about your love for whatever that may be.

That said, my next suggestion is to make a commitment to not take for granted *any* of the relationships that you hold near and dear to your heart. By doing so, you can use this standard as a guide for fostering wonderful relationships that can impact your life forever.

By taking this approach, you can show the rest of your organization that relationships can be established and fostered in a professionally personal way. It goes without saying that you should never overshare something confidential or put your friends in a unique place because of the information that you know—be sincere and authentic.

Last but not least in my attempt to provide professional relationship advice is the suggestion that things change, priorities shift, and relationships evolve. You will develop certain relationships at work that require steady time to keep the relationship going. In other cases, you can go years without seeing someone, and the moment you connect again it seems like it was just yesterday that you saw each other. The bond is immediate, and reconnecting is instant. Be careful not to compare your relationship with one friend to any other relationship you have. That bond you have is unique, and it will change over time as priorities change with new life events like having a child, being promoted, getting married, and the list goes on. All of this is okay and is simply part of the evolution of each of your relationships.

Ben Eubanks, the chief research officer at Lighthouse Research & Advisory and author of *Artificial Intelligence for HR* and *Talent Scarcity*, emphasized that it's critical to learn the business through your relationships. These business relationships ensure that you know "what levers I can pull from an HR or talent perspective that will impact the business. Knowing the people of your business enables HR professionals to adapt and helps us align people with the business."

"My HR mentor truly got to know the people that she worked with, and it was magical what she was able to achieve," explained Ben. "There are so many ways an HR professional who knows the people *and* business can make a big difference."

It was important and therapeutic for me to write this section as I believe relationship building has become a lost art in our society, let alone our workplaces. With the advent of social media and texting, people have become lazy in fostering their most important relationships. A quick text or happy birthday wish on social media is not enough for someone important to you. The idea of "popping in on a friend" simply does not happen as spontaneously as it did when it was not as easy for us to communicate with our friends remotely.

Remember to be sincere and authentic with your relationships by checking and demonstrating interest in what they're experiencing. Modeling positive behaviors is one of the best ways your team can learn from you. As we mentioned earlier in this chapter, most people will admit that when they leave a job or retire, the number one thing they miss is the people. The relationships they are referencing are the friends they made over the years.

Part V
Take Action

Chapter 13
Be a Force of Nature

My hope now is that you have conquered the previous sections on thinking differently, being different, and being better, you are now ready to *take action*! It is not enough to just read this book, say that you did, tell all of your friends, and then do nothing with it. Someone that does *HR Like a Boss* is a force of nature, carefully strategizing and planning . . . and then doing what they set out to do. Ultimately, action is required to get things done. Do you know of a highly successful colleague or HR professional that does not take action?

As you know by now, doing *HR Like a Boss* requires a different mindset. Have you ever found yourself noticing an issue that you could help improve, only to shy away from doing anything because it's "not my job"? Unfortunately, this aversion to taking action in areas of concern where impact can be made is all too common in the workplace. It may not be in *anyone's* job description, but a boss takes it upon themselves to do what they can to fix the problem.

With extraordinary pride, I share this personal story about my oldest and only son, Will. When he was just 9 years old, he started mowing lawns for our next-door neighbor (thanks, Colleen). He had a true passion for it and loved the simplicity and immediate gratification of the before and after of his work. As each summer passed, other neighbors recognized Will's work and his one-yard lawn service began to grow. Eventually, he named the company Will Do Lawn Service and came up with the catchy slogan "So you don't have to" to pun with the name.

A couple of years later, Will lost two of his biggest yards before the start of his mowing season. One of his clients moved, and the new neighbor who bought Will's client's house had a personal relationship with his lawn service. The other neighbor purchased a lawn-mower so that his father-in-law could mow his yard. I had never seen my son so devastated. He took great pride in his work and struggled to comprehend why someone would not use his service. On top of that, just a few months before the summer mowing season, Will had invested in (with his own money) a stand-up Wright mower. He had aspired to buy this type of mower because of the precision of its cut, the mowing lines that it made, and the fact that the YouTubers he followed suggested it was the best mower used by professional landscapers.

As a result, Will was at a bit of a crossroads with his little business. He had invested in the equipment and had the resources to grow his customer base, but Will was thrown a curveball by unexpectedly losing a couple of his customers. When you have five total customers, losing two of them is a huge deal. It was expected for my then-12-year-old son to be upset and frustrated.

Once Will got through the shock and frustration of losing those precious customers, the two of us sat down and talked through what happened. I asked him several questions centered around how he felt and why he felt that way. In his own heartfelt and simple way, my son shared that he really cared about his business and did not understand why someone would not want to use his lawn service. I still remember that conversation to this day, as it became clear to me then how much he loved mowing lawns and the confidence and pride that came from it.

So I did what I thought was best—hugged him and asked if he was open to a few suggestions on what he could do to rebuild his business.

He wanted to grow and thought it made sense to buy a new mower. However, he did not have a clear plan about how he would acquire new clients and retain the ones he had. In my suggestions to my son, the lesson was that every business needs a well-thought-out and clear plan. I tried to simplify the concept of making a plan like this:

1. Think about it,
2. Talk it out,
3. Write it down,
4. Do it,
5. Cross it off, and
6. Learn from it.

The story of Will Do Lawn Service does have a happy ending. My son's strategy centered around two main things:

» New customers: targeting people who he knew and neighbors who had just moved into the neighborhood and did not have a lawn service, and
» Satisfied customers: reaching out to his existing customer base monthly to make sure they were happy with his service.

My son put together a new flier and passed it out to every household in our neighborhood. As it turns out, he landed two new yards

Figure 13–1. Will Do Lawn Service logo

to mow weekly along with several mulch jobs. Will Do Lawn Service was back up and running, and my son was beaming with excitement.

What can we draw from this experience? Maybe, just maybe, you might be doing what you think is best in your role and career, but you lack a clear and concise plan that achieves the personal and professional goals that you desire. In addition, it is not typical for an individual to write out a career plan or an individual business plan, especially for someone in the field of human resources.

Value = Growth + Innovation + Profitability + Transparency

Before drafting your plan, let's dive into the concept of value for a moment and the formula that we suggest you use to increase the value of your organization. Value is a concept that seems very straightforward but is the Holy Grail of business ownership. At the core, one of the primary reasons entrepreneurs start a business is to make money. Now, I hope after reading this book that corporate America will take a more purpose-driven mindset instead of seeking such greedy outcomes. It is, however, critical for HR to understand and embrace the principles behind what makes a business valuable and how to maximize this value.

If your business is publicly traded, this feels a bit easier because there is a regular trading platform that sets a share price for your company, meaning your company's valuation is clear. For those who work in a privately held business, the valuation of your company is far more challenging to determine as the market price is not set on a regular basis. On top of that, many owners of privately held companies keep finances close to the vest and do not share this information with their leadership team or employees. To me, not sharing financials can end up being a mysterious, dark secret in the evolving dynamic between ownership, managers, and employees.

This reference to secrets reminds me of the tragic story for die-hard Cleveland Browns fans when Art Modell left town to take his struggling, iconic sports franchise to Baltimore. Most of the front office staff, coaches, and players had no idea that this was happening and, in some cases, found out about it while listening to sports talk radio or in the newspaper. Why did Art Modell leave Cleveland? He was upside down financially, had a horrible stadium lease deal, and had limited support from local officials to build a new stadium. Art Modell shopped his sports franchise around and found a suitor in the city of Baltimore who welcomed him with open arms after their community lost the Colts to Indianapolis ten years earlier.

It is not often that an ownership group is completely transparent about the financial hardships they may be facing as it is often perceived that owners are rich and have endless means. In some cases, this is true, but in many instances, business owners are struggling financially and may even rob Peter to pay Paul to make payroll or pay suppliers. It is an unpleasant place to be in, but many owners find themselves in this situation with no idea how exactly they got there.

What You Can (and Should) Do

Here's an opportunity for HR: find a way to help your CEO and executive team ensure that the business's strategic plan will increase the value of your business through an intentional purpose and firm-wide knowledge and transparency about growth, profit, and innovation. I have seen the value of this work firsthand. In the initial five years, Willory experienced supergrowth and received rewards for our success but found itself cash-poor and struggling financially because of making investments in people and new service offerings that took longer than expected to yield results.

The first tenet that helps ownership and shareholders maximize the valuation of their business is growth, pure and simple. When an organization grows, there are greater opportunities to improve operations, do more things with resources, and add new products, services, and staff. In addition, growth can suggest that your company is well-run, or that the market requires whatever product or service your company is selling. There is an association of growth with winning. People, customers, suppliers, and partners like to be part of a winning team. The ability to drive in new customers and pad your top line is a key step in helping to improve the value of your business.

The human resources function can help an organization grow by providing clarity of the business purpose, alignment of the culture, attracting of the right talent, calibration of organizational and personal goals, and development of employees through training on the desired behaviors and skills. With this, growth expedites the business valuation of your company. The more your company grows, the greater the multiple that is used by business valuation experts. For example, a business that yields a one million dollars per year earnings before interest, taxes, depreciation, and amortization (EBITDA) will typically see a multiple of five times compared to a business with a ten million dollars per year EBITDA which will typically yield a six-times multiple. These multiples of five times and six times are examples and can differ from industry to industry. This continues as your company's EBITDA continues to grow.

One way for a company to grow and accelerate the value of their business is through innovation and differentiation to better serve their customers and employees. Innovation can result in new product lines, improved manufacturing processes, stellar customer service, attraction and retention philosophies, protected assets, and proprietary methods for developing software or products. Developing or owning something different and better than what your competitors offer can create a distinct competitive advantage. It can fuel further innovation, sales growth, and new client acquisition, as well as attract talent into your business when used properly.

The responsibility of creating an environment for collaboration and new ideas is squarely on the shoulders of the human resources profession. Innovation and ideation should be a part of your culture. The opportunity to create new things, make mistakes without consequence, step outside of your comfort zone, challenge the status quo, collaborate across departments, update a legacy process, question a decision made by leadership (or better yet the owner), debunk a we've-always-done-it-this-way process, and share your ideas comes from this type of culture. Of course, the opposite effect is brutally apparent in a culture that thwarts innovation or new thoughts and ideas from everyone in the organization except a select few.

Challenging the status quo is critical for someone doing *HR Like a Boss*—or any kind of boss, really. Someone doing *HR Like a Boss* looks for financial realities in terms of tying activities to revenues and permeates a boss-like mentality throughout the organization. Every business and business unit can point to at least one and often several cases of "we do it this way because this is just how we do it." It is a mentality that makes challenging the status quo feel somewhat risky.

One area of influence that HR can use to fill an organization with innovation is a real and effective diversity, equity, inclusion, and belonging (DEIB) plan. DEIB is a cornerstone for innovative thought, collaboration, and acceptance of new ideas. With the vast majority of sensible people acknowledging the positive impact of doing the right thing, one can expect customers to be more loyal, and employees to be more attracted to companies that inherently live with this mindset. Simply put, it is the right thing to do.

Don't get me wrong, I am not blind to the idea that some may call me a privileged white male. I have not experienced the oppression that many have experienced. However, I know that I can make a big difference in a small way. My choice to lead by example when it comes to including people who are different from me, be curious to learn about and understand differences, and provide equitable pay no matter the race or gender is a major part of that difference.

As you develop and implement your DEIB strategies and plans, consider how your organization will ensure that innovation and collaboration take place across all people and departments to advance your organization.

Innovation coming from a diverse and inclusive culture will increase the chances of our next cornerstone—increasing your business's value and profitability. No detail is too small when it comes to an organization's finances. Diving into the details of the components that make up the revenue, cost of goods sold (COGS), and indirect expenses will help you and all your employees understand the financial viability of your organization. It is critical to understand your organization and industry metrics when it comes to comparing revenue to COGS, COGS to indirect expense, and revenue to profitability. These ratios will help you set the year-over-year benchmarks to achieve financial success.

Let's dive into how HR can help in these financial areas. In terms of revenue, your organization's strategy and execution around sales and marketing will most directly impact income. You can ensure that the sales and marketing teams have an effective strategy, clear processes, concise branding, productive staff, professional development, and aligned messaging. In addition, ask if these teams are considering the market conditions and how your customers are reacting to your pricing, product quality, and service approach. Do you have an effective and aligned sales incentive compensation in place?

As you investigate the COGS, the details of where the costs lie typically fall on the operations, research & development (R&D), procurement, and finance teams. Thoroughly examining every cost down to the penny ensures that your organization is looking under every rock to deliver quality products or services in the most cost-effective way. It is of utmost importance to have effective collaboration among these teams with process-oriented, quality-driven, and financially savvy employees. By understanding the impact of your organization's COGS, you will be armed with the intelligence and insight to help your operations, R&D, procurement, and finance teams meet or, better yet, exceed their aspirations to deliver high-quality work at the right price. That way, your customers will see the value your company delivers and purchase your products or services.

The final aspect of the profit equation is the indirect expense. To me, the indirect expense cost associated with employees should be the number one reason that human resources is intimately involved and properly invested in indirect costs. Why is that? The totality of employees' costs—including wages, bonuses, perks, health and welfare insurance, retirement benefits, and payroll taxes—typically outpaces all other indirect expenses by a large margin. For that reason, it is critical that HR closely monitors, strategizes, and calibrates additional investments in wages and benefits. More often than not, the most difficult decisions made by a management team involve reducing staff, cutting wages, or eliminating benefits. Every department's people budget should be challenged to ensure every new hire will deliver value for their department and the organization. Taking the time to ensure a thorough examination of the return on investment (ROI) for each new hire along with each department's existing team members will drastically reduce the life-altering and organizational culture-changing decision to lay off employees because the company did not produce enough value to sustain the level of expense associated with employees.

Of course, there is a litany of other expense areas that HR should be aware of such as technology and software, travel, advertising, legal, marketing, and insurance. Every dollar spent in these areas should deliver efficiency, compliance, or effectiveness to each departments' budget. When looking at your organization's expenses, consider its relationship and ratio to revenue, COGS, and profitability.

It is important to consider that many people take business very seriously and view making money as a cutthroat reality. This reality is difficult for some to accept. If that is you, take the approach of understanding where this money-hungry businessperson is coming from and explore if they are willing to consider a different, people-before-profit perspective. If you do not study and better understand the motives behind the importance of money, you will find yourself questioning your purpose on every morning commute for the rest of your business career.

HR's clearest task in this valuation is finding and developing talent for the organization within a budget the company can afford. Someone who does *HR Like a Boss* understands each role within a specific department *and* what the department does to contribute to profitability. Through this understanding, HR, who is often tasked with finding the best people, is able to find the pieces that fit the organization.

HR's command of profitability and the growth path of the company is fundamental in dictating the number of people the company employs, what they can be paid (including incentives), job duties and responsibilities, and so on. All of this depends on whether or not the organization is growing and on the answer to the question, "Are we profitable?"

Earlier on, we highlighted Lauren Rudman, *HR Like a Boss* extraordinaire. She put HR's place in the scheme of business growth and profitability this way: "I don't think that HR people should be naive to understand that HR is viewed and budgeted in many organizations as a cost center. I mean, I don't directly make the company money. The people on the frontlines are the reason why I have a job and, of course, why HR professionals have a job. That's why it's so important, and really our responsibility is to go out there and see the people who really do make our company money. What do they do and how do they do it?"

Someone doing *HR Like a Boss* helps the organization do boss-like things such as driving innovation for revenue growth, evaluating COGS, and collaborating on profit-inducing ideas. In turn, they help the organization track and measure *everything* and its value to the business. Not everything is tied directly to revenue, but how much value does back-office support deliver to producers? Measuring the actual profitability of a support system of both people and systems may not be easy, but someone doing *HR Like a Boss* finds a way.

Closer to home with their own job duties and activities, HR's view of hiring and retention should have a growth and profit perspective. This includes helping departments define the desired outcomes for their positions and finding the means and metrics to measure them. As we said before, there's no bigger investment than people and accompanying salaries—make sure you help your hiring managers understand how to determine success. HR helps the company measure the investment in people on an individual basis to ensure each employee contributes positively to the top and bottom lines. Every job, at first, will be an investment. But, in the long term, every job needs to be profitable and have a demonstrable, measurable impact on the business.

We need the support systems to free up our revenue-generating employees so that revenue exceeds the support staff investment. At Willory, we run a value matrix for each one of our positions, including nonrevenue support roles, that tells us if we are getting value that exceeds the investment. Effectively doing this provides our HR team the perspective to evaluate every single position, including those in the HR department.

When HR understands where the business makes money, how profitable it is, and the activities that drive growth, HR can be highly influential in these areas by developing programs and aligning employees to improve the key financial viability of the company. That's a boss move! So how do you do that?

Once HR has a grasp of your organization's Accounting 101, take it to the people. An employee who understands profitability can help the organization reach profitability through proactive efforts. To help manage the unfortunate circumstances of a layoff, transparency allows employees to know *why* some roles are unable to be retained—the business was not performing. The net result is the same as someone is still out of a job . . . but by educating employees about profitability, the employee can (hopefully) help turn things around, or at worst, leave with their dignity intact. This can't be understated; getting fired or losing a job can be devastating—as people who love people, someone doing *HR Like a Boss* wants the individual to come to terms with the unfortunate situation, remain positive, and find alternative employment relatively quickly. This reinforces the importance of HR helping employees understand the business, its profitability, and growth (or lack thereof). Creating employee access to key components and collaboration around profitability not only encourages individuals to be their own boss, but also lets employees know the hard realities that may lead to having to separate from a good employee.

Beyond just the reality that folks understand why bad things happen, let's look at the numerous benefits that come about from sharing financial information. Someone doing *HR Like a Boss* knows that financial transparency creates a team of employees that are all invested in the company's success and empowered to impact revenues on an individual basis. Rolling out knowledge of revenue reality makes everyone more conscientious about investments and how money is spent. Much like a budget at home, if everyone, including the kids, has an idea of what can (and can't) be spent, the family unit will operate more effectively (and peacefully). Employees who know the realities of EBITDA can make better decisions.

Therefore, it is important to emphasize the critical nature of an organization being transparent to its employees, customers, and shareholders. In HR's case, protecting employees is its top priority. All too often, employees are surprised by major decisions that are made within S&P 500 employers all the way down to a mom-and-pop small business. Why is that? In my view, it is one simple thing. Leadership does not believe that its employees can handle bad news. As a result, they believe this bad news will scare off their employees. This is not the right approach, but it took me time to learn through some challenging lessons. Finding the level of transparency that works for your organization is an imperative responsibility of HR. Some companies can share everything, and others, especially those who are publicly traded, need to, per legal restrictions, ensure they're sharing the right information with the right people at the right time.

My Own (Lack of) Transparency

At Willory, it took me more than five years to realize the benefits of transparency when it came to profitability. Not because I was buying yachts or fancy cars—but rather, I was trying to insulate the team from the (worrisome) ups and downs of a start-up business. Some years we would throw off a lot of cash and others we struggled to turn a profit. I was afraid my team would focus on the occasional bad year and panic when the reality is that the good years are what carry you through an off year.

A few years ago, I found myself getting irritated at my team for not caring as much as I did about the firm's financial performance. This is when I realized that there was no way for them to care as much as me. How could they care about something they didn't understand, something I wasn't providing any visibility into? At the same time, blogs popped up about the benefits of sharing financials with employees and I even observed a client's quarterly financials in their lobby during a visit. In addition, a financial and accounting advisor of mine, Matt Soful, really pushed me in this direction based upon the principles outlined in *Profit First* by Mike Michalowicz. It is a book about transforming your business from a cash-eating monster to a money-making machine.

So, I started gradually sharing Willory's company financials with its employees.

With help, our team went through the basics of a profit and loss (P&L) statement and started to dig into the Willory financials. I immediately saw that my team was making better decisions because I empowered them to be bosses in their own disciplines. This also paid off when the pandemic hit in 2020. The team was able to see what we were facing, and what we could and could not sustain. It was a difficult time as we made some tough decisions that impacted the lives of people that we cared about, but the team had a better understanding of the realities of the situation and why we did what we did.

In some cases, the unknowns of what life would be like in early 2020 forced our hand, making decisions that we put off for too long and cutting some expenses that we should have made well before having our hands forced to do so.

Chapter 14
Treat Your Job/Function Like a Business

To make earth-shattering, move-mountains changes, you must employ the first principle of doing *HR Like a Boss* . . . take ownership. The easiest way for me to convey how to do this is to think of your job as its own business. Whether you are a senior in college on your school's student Society for Human Resource Management (SHRM) chapter board, a part-time payroll processor, an HR manager with three direct reports and responsibilities for a business line with one hundred employees, or a chief human resources officer (CHRO) of a *Fortune* 100 company, you must look at what you do with a boss-like mentality.

How do you do that?

First, you must establish your personal stakes in what it is you're doing; this is *my own* business mindset. Looking at your job, role, or department as your own business changes everything. Mind you, you do not have to write up official corporate papers or form an LLC or S corp. However, you should draw up a strategic business plan for your role. Doing *HR Like a Boss* means you will be entrepreneurial and treat your role as a business. There are countless business plans online. For one tailored to those aspiring to do *HR Like a Boss*, check out www.hrlikeaboss.com.

In your so-called "business" plan, you must answer several questions that notable entrepreneurs and tycoons had to address when building their own businesses, including the following:

» What is the purpose of my business?
» What core values must we live by?
» Who is my customer? What do they need? What are their pain points?
» Who are the people that will help me?
» What are your core processes?
» What are my business strengths?
» Where are my biggest opportunities for improvement?
» What problems or gaps exist?
» What is my business's biggest threat or impediment?

Writing your initial business plan should be an iterative journey with many stops, starts, and head scratches over weeks (if not months) of personal reflection and thought-provoking moments, beyond the normal realm of pondering, in-depth soul-searching, and constant consideration. Whew.

As a part of that process, take a moment to reach out to an HR or business professional you respect and aspire to be like someday. Schedule a time to meet with them to learn by asking many questions and showing them your *HR Like a Boss* business plan. Be prepared for that meeting. Ask them for critiques, edits, and suggestions.

To provide some additional depth about your strategic business plan, employ the following *HR Like a Boss* strategic formula:

HR Like a Boss plan =
    Purposeful commitment +
    People-centric +
    Produce consistently +
    Process continuity +

Profitable components +

Personal characteristics

Let's dive into the components of the *HR Like a Boss* plan:

Purposeful Commitment

First, every business needs a clearly defined purpose. The purpose of a business correlates to the importance of location to real estate.

Location, location, location is the same as purpose, purpose, purpose.

Make sure your purpose is simple (two to four words) and incredibly aspirational. To me, there has been a (rightful) shift away from the use of the word "mission" to "purpose" recently. Your organization's purpose isn't just an external branding phrase but should inform the decisions employees at all levels make.

Willory's purpose is "we empower people." It is aspirational and something that we will never fully achieve as we will never empower every single person in the world. But we certainly are going to try! In addition, we have core values to ensure our team members are aligned with how we are going about achieving our purpose. Our core values are the following:

- » Passionate desire to improve.
- » Greatness through accountability.
- » Enthusiasm in all we do.
- » Seek to understand.
- » Live by the Golden Rule.

Our purpose aligned with our core values sets the foundation for our culture, which drives results for our customers and provides a family-oriented feel for our team. Additionally, core values offer a guidepost for everyone within the company. They should be shared with new hires, departmental colleagues, and other employees and serve as a constant reminder of what is expected and what is non-negotiable within your organization and culture. One of Willory's directors and a leader in developing our updated core values explains how we hire and evaluate our team with a question she asks herself: "Do we have the right team members that align to our core values and purpose to achieve our business goals?"

While getting your purpose in writing—even if it starts on the back of a napkin, then gets plastered all over your cubical or home office—is crucial. Commitment to your organization's purpose is also important. The DNA of your business, the people that support you, and your stakeholders must be 110 percent committed to the purpose in their actions. If not, the whole world and most importantly your customers will see right through this marketing spin, just like Max eventually saw through his fib-happy father, Fletcher, in the 1997 box office hit *Liar Liar.* You cannot fool people; well maybe you can a time or two, but eventually, they will figure you out to be as much of a fraud as Jim Carrey's character.

It's important to remember that your values and purpose need to inspire and serve the organization. If, over time, you find your values and purpose aren't aligned with the organization, you need to take the time to review them. Values can be removed from your list of company values because they become a "given" or because they no longer support the strategic initiatives. Sometimes, you might realize you left something important off with a revamp. Values aren't set in stone and should be given the chance to live.

A purposeful commitment is the most important intention that an organization can have. As was previously mentioned, the purpose is as important to a business as the location is to real estate. Remember these three words when grappling with the importance of and charting the course to develop and maintain your organization's why:

Purpose. Purpose. Purpose.

People-Centric

After your purpose is clearly intact, we will center in on people as a part of your strategic plan and the plan's execution. So, taking a "people-centric" approach to everything you do is critical in your business plan. Think about a turnaround in a department after a struggling or troublesome manager is replaced with an effective manager. People make the world go round and are front and center to HR's responsibility within an organization.

Being people-centric should be obvious and likely is the one pillar most HR professionals identify with. We have all heard numerous HR thought leaders share that HR needs to put the "human" back in human resources. Simply put, people make a business succeed or fail. It is HR's responsibility to look at every person that its business impacts and make sure that they achieve the desired outcomes. The simplest way to round out this idea is to encourage you to talk to your stakeholders, including team members, colleagues, executives, vendors, customers, and shareholders. Ask them questions and truly listen to what they say. In those conversations, you will learn valuable lessons on what your so-called "business" needs and how to support your customers best.

Speaking of valuable lessons, in 2012, I had the pleasure of connecting with Kris Dunn, who has become a great sounding board for me regarding HR and business. He provides an incredibly unique and thought-provoking perspective on business, HR, and life. Kris has many accolades and titles, including CHRO and being the founder of HR Capitalist, Fistful of Talent (FOT), and BOSS Training Series. He is also the author of the popular HR book, *The 9 Faces of HR*. Before Kris was a world-renowned author, he came to Cleveland to do a wildly entertaining presentation about his 9-box theory. During his pitch, it became apparent that Kris loved basketball as much if not more than HR, and we enjoyed a memorable LeBron-James-led Cavs win versus Kris's Atlanta

Hawks. In Kris's view, someone doing *HR Like a Boss* examines the people-centric mantra as a harmonious balance between employee and employer. "HR's purpose serves two masters, you have to have one foot on both sides of the fence," explained Dunn. "You need to help your business get great results while helping employees in a people-friendly, progressive manner. These are not mutually exclusive—you can and should do both!" He went on to say that "if you lose sight of either side, individual or company, you get out of balance and you become a mediocre HR pro . . . not a Boss at all." It is indeed as Kris said, "more art than science," but for you to do *HR Like a Boss* means that you need to find a way to achieve balance and "avoid bias towards the business while being too empathic for an employee which overruns you prohibiting good decisions." To Kris's point, finding that balance is critical.

Put your people first. If you do not, someone else will!

Produce Consistently

As a direct tie to being people-centric, let's dive into how HR can help its organization produce consistently. It must be clear what you are trying to accomplish in your business and how you will achieve it. It is all about clearly defining your goals and desired outcomes, in writing, by answering the following questions:

» What are the outcomes or goals you are trying to achieve?
» How are you going to do it?
» What is your process to achieve it?
» How will you document it?
» What will you measure along the way to monitor your progress?
» How will you continuously improve it?
» How will you hold yourself accountable to achieve those outcomes or goals?

Beyond your own business, I have found that the owner of that function does not always seek HR's role in achieving productivity within a business. If that happens to you, dig in by approaching the manager or VP who is responsible to understand why they are avoiding HR's help. As a product of this avoidance, HR is not always included in critical discussions. Ask the leaders of a particular department struggling to reach its performance metrics or find a team filled with turmoil and drama. Then, offer to get involved in helping to create solutions. I am not suggesting that HR should be involved in every employee issue (that would be impossible and terribly inefficient). However, you must ensure your managers and leaders are equipped with the skills, tools, temperament, and experience to navigate the twists and turns of employee development properly and effectively.

Once we have a course of action to achieve consistent productivity and truly understand how different aspects of what your "business" does impact your organization's revenue, cost of goods sold (COGS), and indirect expense, it is up to you, the leadership team, managers, and your employees to produce results consistently. The financial bottom line of your company and the well-being of your employees depend on it. As a result, you, your team, and your employees should have a solid grasp and know as much about their impact on the company's profit and loss (P&L) as your controller and CFO do.

Process Continuity

I must admit that I personally struggle the most with being consistent about repeating my processes day after day. I don't know if I look at doing things the same way over and over again as mundane or if there is a loftier reason that I struggle with it, like, my entrepreneurial nature can't get comfortable to get granular enough.

But it is crucial as I strive to create clarity and consistency in the most essential processes to stabilize and ultimately scale my business. Understanding my personal shortcomings, I took the "leverage my strengths and hire to my weaknesses" advice I have heard hundreds of times from those much more intelligent than me.

As a quick aside, let's not underestimate the importance of working with colleagues, partners, or vendors who are more skilled and experienced than you to accomplish the goals you set for yourself.

As a result, my advice or two cents worth of guidance on process continuity is more of a potpourri of counsel that I have received over the years from those much more skilled and equipped in the field of process improvement.

The first step to creating efficient and continuous processes across your organization is to determine a vision for what process continuity looks like for your organization. This step will require taking a giant step back and freeing yourself from the confines of thinking "this is the way" we do things in order to paint the picture of how it should be done. Nothing you currently do regarding your people, processes, and technology should hold you back from creating your ideal future state for your key business processes.

Once you have a vision created of your quintessential state for your key business processes, the next step is to dive into your current processes and complete a thorough discovery exercise to examine all your business-critical processes. These processes should include all vital business activities that do the following:

» Generate cash,
» Spend cash,
» Are critical to how your business operates, and
» Define the core aspects (two to three) of each department of your organization.

Since this is a book about HR, attracting talent, paying employees, and retaining talent are examples of three processes to examine how they are being done, where the bottlenecks exist, what opportunities can we leverage, and the risk factors that exist.

Then, it is time to write all of your examinations about these business-critical processes down and consolidate them into a one-page description. I recommend starting with a simple explanation and comparing it to the ideal future state that you set out at the beginning of this process continuity journey.

Once you have examined the duplication of effort, inefficiencies, areas to leverage, and opportunities for improvement, document what the process should look like and determine the steps necessary to reach that ideal state. Then, create a project plan and put a team together to get there.

In order to create true process continuity, all leaders and departments should follow a similar procedure and then compare the results. Do not overthink it or, more importantly, overdo it. Simplify each process into a one-page document. If your team or a colleague with advanced PowerPoint or Visio skills wants to show off their talents with charts, graphs, and screenshots, let them loose. But those visuals that they create should be references to support your simple one-page process continuity document.

Last but not least, your final step in creating process continuity is quantifying the metrics (whether that is a goal, quota, or ratio) that you expect to achieve from the key business processes that you and your organization deem critical. Baked into the number is understanding the steps required to achieve your goal and quantifying the ratio of each step along the way. Using another HR-related metric, how much do we need to spend in recruiting advertisement dollars to generate enough quality candidates to meet our hiring goals?

I know it seems like a lot, and defining and refining processes is the can that gets kicked down the road. Fight the urge to make it perfect and instead keep it simple. Set aside time to make it happen. Then, measure your results to gauge your progress. Once you have perfected your processes, show the other departments in your organization how to make it happen. Now, that is *HR Like a Boss.*

Profitable Components

Gaining this financial knowledge will help you explore the profitable components and all that your "business," along with every employee and department, does or does not do to make your organization profitable. To me, profitability is the scorecard of a business—including someone doing *HR Like a Boss*. Otherwise, your business is just a hobby or a company that will not be around for very long. Profitability in your business comes from how you, your team, and your employees impact the bottom line. In the competitive business world, many leaders obsessively seek objective, fact-based data to help them make decisions. It can be difficult to measure the impact of an influential culture, professional development, or training investments. That said, it is up to you to figure out the financial impact of what you are doing or looking to implement. Without them, your initiatives will get shot down, or worse, they won't receive the executive-level support needed to make a true impact.

This is one of the reasons why some of the diehard, old-school, non-HR professionals that I know can justify an "I hate HR" stance, as they have not been shown a quantified, measurable impact from an effective HR team. So, it is paramount that you start to measure the dollars and cents and cultural impact of the things that make a bottom-line difference from HR, including the following:

- » having kick-ass hiring,
- » saving money by curbing high turnover,
- » enhancing the employee experience through an innovative onboarding process,
- » increasing productivity through training,
- » minimizing waste through process efficiency reducing costs due to cutting edge benefit offerings,
- » increasing shareholder value through a personalized customer service model, and

» displaying topline revenue growth due to alignment between sales and marketing.

Personal Characteristics

Once you have examined, dissected, and brainstormed your purpose, people, productivity, processes, and profit for your strategic plan, it's time to look within yourself. The objective of the personal characteristics is to leverage your strengths and to be mindful of your weaknesses or blind spots. We could devote an entire chapter to just this topic if not a whole book. However, I am not in the business of telling you or anyone else how to act. This duty is limited to my responsibility as a parent, which I am blessed to not have to do that often with my kids.

It is up to you to find an employer, group of friends, and support system that you are comfortable being yourself with while also being open to input, feedback, and suggestions. I am not trying to turn the field of HR into a bunch of *HR Like a Boss* robots. That statement could not be further from the truth. My encouragement about personal characteristics is to bring out the best in others by being your true, genuine self. That coupled with wanting to get better, build solid relationships, and make an impact will chart you on a course to success.

As it has been part of my M.O. throughout the entire book, I shall make another eighties reference. From 1985 to 2015, David Letterman would report a Top Ten list on each one of his broadcasts. Letterman's Top Ten lists began as a riff on how people, especially men, love lists. The first Top Ten list was "Top Ten Words That Almost Rhyme with Peas." The goal of our list is not to show off our rhyming skills but instead to showcase the characteristics of amazingly awesome HR. Our list came out of a culmination of several surveys and hundreds of discussions with stellar HR pros.

Our list is so unique that we added an asterisk to the title. Careful examination of our list will tell you why.

The Top Ten* Personal Characteristics of Someone Who Does *HR Like a Boss*

Takes Ownership

Be enterprising and embrace responsibility for everything that you can influence in your HR role and the business. Look beyond to see where you should make an impact and embrace where you *could* make an impact. Instead of being hands-off in areas that aren't necessarily in your job description, get involved where you can make a difference. As an HR professional, be a model for your organization and take responsibility. Owners can't rely on excuses as the buck stops with them—do the same and develop and implement solutions!

Loves What They Do

You must love what you do, and in HR, this includes working with people! HR is a profession that not only requires an understanding of the dynamic between employees and the employer, but that you love them both and are passionate about making the best workplace possible, despite human flaws.

Leads by Example

A leader is not only someone who others gravitate to and follow but, more importantly, exemplifies and models the behaviors that serve as an example of doing things *the right way*. A leader gets the most out of their people to transcend and elevate the organization.

Thinks Strategically

A strategic HR professional considers a large range of factors when considering changes that would impact their company and its people. Being strategic means seeing the *big picture* and the long-term ramifications of acting versus not acting. Being strategic means examining in-depth the potential outcomes before acting.

Shapes Company's Vision

HR must understand the why of your business and effectively, clearly, and concisely communicate the vision of your company in both the written and spoken word. Doing *HR Like a Boss* requires you to create clarity where confusion may exist when standards are not clear or accountability to a company's core values seems misaligned.

Acts Ethically

An upstanding, ethical individual possesses a moral compass with a purposeful true north. To be a trusted HR professional, you must be transparent and honest. Doing *HR Like a Boss* requires trust, openness, honesty, and transparency in all of your activities.

Demonstrates Resiliency

The world and its circumstances are ever-changing and evolving. HR professionals must be resilient and agile to adapt when things change. HR professionals understand the dynamic between an employee and an employer and recognize that every possible real-world situation doesn't have a solution found in an employee handbook. Every situation is not black and white; doing *HR Like a Boss* requires being exceptional at working in the gray areas of work and life.

Lives with Authenticity

It is easier to develop relationships and establish trust when you are truly real and trustworthy. An HR professional needs to be genuine, real, and sincere to maximize relationships with employees and peers.

Explores Emotions

Marc Brackett encourages people to be an "emotion scientist," which is someone who is comfortable and capable with their own emotions and has heightened self-awareness. Just as importantly, these high EQ people are mindful and aware of other people's emotions and can mix empathy and facts as each situation warrants.

Focuses on Purpose

An HR professional should be intentional—with their work and how they carry themselves. A clear and evident answer behind actions reveals the actions' what and why—being purposeful starts by focusing on the why mindset and recognizing the greater good that your employees and company can offer to society and your community.

Learns Constantly

Within each professional relationship, from long-term with a CEO to short-term with a candidate in an interview, the best HR professionals are curious. Don't stop asking great questions—listen, evaluate, and follow up to ensure you understand the answers! Approach each conversation as an opportunity to learn.

Exudes Confidence

Be professionally defiant and don't assume "it can't be done," but rather find a new and creative way to achieve business goals. You will need endurance and persistence, but what can't be done just hasn't been accomplished . . . yet.

What's Your Perspective?

So, what do you think? Is the list comprehensive enough? Is it too much to expect from one person? Did you start to think about how the characteristics relate to other HR pros you know or, more importantly, did you start to do your self-assessment? Or, maybe you thought of several different, more personal characteristics or attributes of someone doing *HR Like a Boss*, which is totally cool.

I would love to get your perspective, and we developed a really cool tool to help you assess yourself on the *HR Like a Boss* scorecard as well as provide your suggestions on additional qualities of amazingly awesome HR professionals. In less than five minutes, you can assess yourself on *HR Like a Boss* personal characteristics. I hope it helps you achieve amazingly awesome HR.

Chapter 15
My Accountability Journey

After you have pulled together your *HR Like a Boss* plan, consider establishing personal accountability to ensure that you implement the plan you diligently set for yourself. To do so, take a moment to consider your accountability journey, the people in your life that have formed your view of personal responsibility, and the real-life situations that shaped how you currently feel and react when you hear the word "accountable." To some, this is a complicated topic to discuss as well as a place where they can get stuck in their own personal development.

Allow me to share my accountability journey. Having two diametrically different parents who provided tough love in their own way; a hard-nosed and highly competitive college golf coach; several hard-charging, corporate-first minded (and sometimes micromanaging) bosses; a loving but at times incredibly direct wife; and a few no-nonsense coaches and advisors, my willingness to be coached and held to task has most certainly been an evolution that has landed in an incredible place due to those previously mentioned mentors, personal experience, and intense education on this subject. In the past, there is no doubt that I have bucked the concept of accountability with a pristine personal view that "I was right, and you were wrong." On top of that, there are some childhood memories of getting scolded or in trouble for things that kids just do. Over my entire lifetime, my tolerance for personal accountability developed and most recently matured to a place of peace and understanding. From that, I developed an "I don't want to get in trouble" mindset, causing me to work hard, be careful with my decisions, and perform at a high level to ensure praise over reprimand.

As a result, I found myself struggling to receive feedback that was critical to my work, performance, or character. In part, holding this viewpoint caused me to quit a corporate job, in which I had performed at a very high level and had a tremendous amount of success, to be my own boss. I didn't know it then, but hindsight tells me that I was running away from accountability in doing so. The reasons were numerous and included my lack of comfort with critical feedback and receiving critiques from superiors, coaches, and mentors who were not perfectly skilled in effectively delivering their opinions to create safety and promote an open, two-way dialogue. It was more important to me to "be" right rather than to get "it" right. In other words, I wanted to win more than I wanted to, honestly, get things right.

Because of my foibles, I felt uncomfortable holding others accountable. Since I did not like critical feedback myself, I would always ask myself, "How can I hold others accountable if it makes me feel uncomfortable?" So I avoided it or likely did a less-than-stellar job during tough conversations. Not to mention, I built up the impending meeting to address an issue or discuss a difficult situation and often retreated on my true feelings to not make the other person feel how I felt for so many years.

When my firm retooled our core values, I found an internal conflict. How can we have one of our core values be "greatness through accountability" while I was not 100 percent comfortable giving and receiving feedback myself? So, I asked some really close friends and advisors, had some in-depth conversations with my business coach, and read several business-focused self-help books.

Thanks to all of that and much more that I won't bore you with, I am now at peace with receiving critical and constructive feedback and being held accountable for one simple reason. My approach is not to take any of what is shared with me personally, create safety so people always feel safe to share anything with me, and seek to understand my counterparts in communication, especially when they come at me aggressively or feel defensive about the subject matter. I was able to change my mindset and run toward accountability successfully.

Sweet, Sweet Accountability

I say all of this to make the point that I now love accountability. As a result of that willingness to receive criticism, feedback, and strong opinions, I am comfortable delivering tough news and have learned to be properly prepared, direct, and fact-based with a keen eye on how I deliver the message and how the other person is receiving what I am sharing.

Once you have recounted your own accountability story, recognize where you stand regarding this subject; then, develop a plan to improve and grow. Begin your journey of setting self-paced milestones or benchmarks to touch base on that must be in your calendar to ensure progress is being made to the plan you set. You can go one step further and establish a board of trusted advisors that you meet with quarterly to review your business plan. If you need help, consider joining an *HR Like a Boss* community to surround yourself with like-minded HR professionals looking to make an impact. All of this is paramount to help you measure your successes and failures and track the progress that you are making on achieving the goals set for your purpose, people, production, processes, and profit.

Chapter 16
Operationalize Your Plan

So, we have a plan and understand the items we can measure that truly make an impact on the employees and our organization. Now, it is time to operationalize your plan. The first place to start is an empty conference room (or your home office) with a whiteboard, a dry erase marker, and about ninety minutes of clear mental space with no distractions. Put your phone away and close your laptop. Think about the top one to three items that you want to improve and believe will have a bottom-line impact on the organization and employee experience. Take the time to

1. List the steps it takes to get what you need to do done,
2. Identify who is involved and how effective they are at what they do,
3. Identify which parts are manual and which are automated, and
4. Identify which parts of the process work and which parts don't.

Then draw visuals of the steps. After that, take a picture (you can use your phone for this). Erase the whiteboard and attack the next item on your list. Stop after ninety minutes.

The next day or so, pull up your picture and create a PowerPoint slide, Word document, Visio diagram, or Canva design that follows along with the visual steps it takes. Then step away from it.

Take what you created and share it with a colleague, business coach, or friend. Tell them about what you are doing and why you are doing it. Ask them for their input and any suggestions.

After that, put it out to your community in a social media post or a directed email to a larger crowd of peers you know and trust. The message should be something like this:

> I am trying to improve the way that I support [INSERT COMPANY NAME] with our [FILL IN THE BLANK] process. I hope to get opinions from those who have done this before or have a very streamlined and efficient process that benefits both your company and your employees.

Now, this assumes that you have an established network. If not, that is okay. Start to build one. All it takes is one person to start a network. Your local Society for Human Resource Management (SHRM) chapter is a great place to start, or you can use your LinkedIn community. Also, you can ask my favorite question to people whom you trust: "Who is the best HR pro that you know and why?" Once you have the name, ask for an introduction. There is a reason that someone said they were the best. Go find out why.

Let's return to making improvements and impacting *your* business. Once you hear back from your network, it is time to refine and change. In making things better and instilling more boss-like aspects into your mindset, you must take the time to strategize on which priorities are most impactful and how you are going to implement these changes. There are four key principles in making a change: proper scope, planning, communication, and reflection.

The scope of change you are going to make must be reasonable and feasible. Too often, people, departments, and companies overpromise and underdeliver on making positive change as they bite off more than they can chew.

As mentioned before, it is essential to settle on no more than three impactful initiatives per calendar year. To that point, only having one item is totally boss-like, assuming it is big and will make a major impact on your role, department, employees, and business.

Once you have your one to three top priorities, develop a plan with the deadlines, timelines, resources needed, people impacted, communication strategy, and risks, then get input and buy-in from your department peers, manager, and leadership. In your plan, you should have a regular meeting cadence (once per week is preferred) in which the team members involved in making these changes are included and clear about their expectations.

As a part of your planning, create an effective communication strategy for the impending changes you plan to make and include everyone involved. One of the key forms of communication is a collaborative discussion with the people impacted by the process or item you are looking to improve. During this discussion, clearly define what you are trying to accomplish and why it is important. Then, ask for input on how a change would impact those involved and any suggestions they have or roadblocks that they see. It is amazing the perspective you will gain from this exercise.

After you follow your plan and implement this flawless new way of doing business with artful communication, schedule time on your calendar to reflect on both the quantifiable and subjective items that will deem your change as a success, failure, or something in between. You will learn so much by taking the time to digest why a particular project was successful and why certain initiatives fail.

Again, being a boss is about owning your role and the positive impacts you can have on your organization. Someone doing *HR Like a Boss* does not have to be an owner in a traditional sense but rather is a person who understands their role and uses their strategic *business* plan to treat their role or department like it is their own company.

Once your plan is complete, share it with a colleague, networking contact, or mentor. Eventually, you should feel empowered to present your plan to your boss and hopefully get their support to showcase your plan with the CEO of your company. If the end goal is to present your plan to the CEO, my guess is you will put more care and feeding with time, energy, thought, and passion into it versus a plan that you show no one and store away in a forgotten electronic file or in the back of your filing cabinet.

Your plan should be dynamic and something that is ever evolving. Your first iteration is only the start, and it should be tweaked, modified, or even overhauled regularly. As things change, so too should you and your plan. As the late Dennis Hopper's character Shooter in the 1986 sports classic, *Hoosiers*, emphatically implored, "don't get caught watchin' the paint dry."[1] A plan is just a piece of paper unless it is implemented, and lessons are learned to modify it along the way.

With your *HR Like a Boss* plan, you are ready to take action. The actions you take are completely up to you and should feel unique to your passions and how you want to do business. Therefore, we will not be giving you a long list of suggestions on how to take action. We will keep it simple with three suggestions:

First, do not be afraid to make a mistake, piss someone off, or do something wrong.

Second, any action is better than no action.

Finally, when taking action, I always lean into some wise counsel I received over the years from several influential people in my life. When doing anything in life, strive to do the best *you* possibly can. Give it your personal best and pour your heart into whatever *it* is. Be careful not to compare your actions to anyone else other than yourself. Taking this approach will alleviate the stress that comes with trying to keep up with some fictitious character of perfection that does not exist and keenly lock in by doing the best you can every day.

1. Anspaugh, David, dir. *Hoosiers.* 1986.

Part VI
Make an Impact

Chapter 17
Putting It All Together

For those who strive to do *HR Like a Boss* and are willing and able to commit to practical and well-thought-out planning and strategizing, the reason we do all of this is to make an impact with a positive outcome. There are many examples of these positives that increase efficiency and improve the employee experience. My favorite of these includes outcomes like

- » Achieving a goal,
- » Completing a task,
- » Saving your company money while adding to your total rewards,
- » Completing a project,
- » Implementing a new HR technology, and
- » Developing a manager who ends up reducing turnover on their team.

All of these have one thing in common: they impacted your employees, company, and possibly the community.

Don't get me wrong, we are sure to make mistakes, skin our knees, or trip over ourselves occasionally in the pursuit of achieving our desired outcomes. We cannot fear failure and allow the terror of the unknown to lead to inaction. Doing nothing is often worse than the wrong action—don't allow yourself to freeze in complacency from a lack of confidence.

How do we get there? How do we take that risk and put ourselves out there?

At the time of writing this book, my purpose is to make an impact (it is not ironic that this section has the same title). These simple three words are the gasoline that fuels my engine. It is my personal purpose in life. I try to keep it simple and consider it with *every single* interaction that I have with anyone in my life from my wife, kids, colleagues, peers, competitors, worthy rivals, and perfect strangers. I have learned the value of this over the years by hearing stories about how someone made such a positive impact on their life and what it took to achieve that profound outcome.

I've heard so many stories about how HR professionals made a difference by helping employees feel valued by being present, actively listening, having empathy, and being clear and direct. More times than not, it is not necessarily the intentional action that those people took that resulted in unparalleled admiration. Instead, the impact was made by how you make people feel and ensuring individuals feel valued.

Over the following few pages, I highlight some of the real-life stories of HR professionals I have showcased in this book who have made a deep and positive impression on those they worked with.

Let's start with Scott Stone, not your average CFO. Scott provides fractional CFO engagements, strategic planning, and organizational development to small-to-mid-sized companies. He lives in the Greater Birmingham area in Alabama and initially worked with one of our *HR Like a Boss*'ers, Kris Dunn, at BellSouth Wireless. When I talked with Scott, he could not define HR and its purpose without referring to his longtime friend: "It is impossible for me to talk about human resources without thinking about Kris Dunn." Scott continued on to say, "The true measure of success of any HR leader is their understanding of their business and what it takes to make it successful."

Scott recalled his first experience with Kris and realized that he was different from the other HR professionals who "flat out sucked," according to Scott. What made him feel so strongly about his HR colleagues at the time was that they acted as an impediment to the business and got in the way of success. Scott realized he needed a change and hired Kris to help deal with a wide array of business challenges that centered around people. "When I first met Kris, he made an immediate positive impression. He was different from the other HR professionals I had worked with in the past. He took a business-first mindset, and he never told the managers, 'You can't do this.'" Scott said that Kris helped them find solutions to their business and people challenges.

As luck would have it, Scott and Kris would work together again about five years later at a turnaround company that needed synergy between the finance and HR teams. Scott inherited a high-margin business with sales growth that lacked profitability and attributed this lack of productivity to a poor-performing workforce. Scott initially hired Kris to help him build a turnaround plan that would drive results for the business. When Scott pitched the people plan that Kris put together to the leadership team, the CEO asked who was behind devising this plan. Scott replied, "Kris Dunn, the best HR professional I have ever worked with in my career." Scott still vividly remembered the CEO's reply to his claim. His CEO matter-of-factly said, "Well, then hire him!"

Kris and Scott implemented their plan to turn around the company. They took a one-new-hire-at-a-time approach to rebuilding the company, changing the culture, and replacing underperforming team members with high performers. In the end, they accomplished their mission as the company was turned around, achieved tremendous sales growth and profitability, and eventually sold for a significant return for the shareholders. Scott attributed much of the success to the plan developed and executed by Kris Dunn.

As Scott wrapped up his comments about Kris and the field of HR, he shared, "Not all HR professionals are ready for a seat at the table." He continued, "If someone is ill-prepared or overzealous to strategically participate on an executive team, they could do tremendous harm and/or crack under the pressure that comes with leading an organization." He felt it took just the right person with the temperament, collaborative approach, and high emotional intelligence to make a real impact.

Scott finished by describing Kris as a "force to be reckoned with, and he set the bar for all other HR pros as he was a true business partner." Now that is *HR Like a Boss.*

Let's shift gears a bit to a resurgence of sorts that resulted from Jennifer Forgac, human resources pro, from Northeast Ohio. I had the pleasure of meeting Jennifer while networking at our local Society for Human Resource Management (SHRM) chapter's regional conference, NOHRC. She is one of the kindest people you will ever meet. Jennifer was assigned to a consulting project for one of our *HR Like a Boss*'ers, Kathy Sullivan. Kathy's whole skill, expertise, knowledge, and approach were displayed when they worked together. Jennifer said, "She is approachable, strategic, well-rounded, respected, and one of the most positive and amazing people that I have ever met." Wow, that is some endorsement. Despite Jennifer's temporary assignment working on Kathy's team, Jennifer was warmly welcomed with open arms and felt like part of the team.

Jennifer recalled Kathy's tenacity and professionalism throughout their engagement. She went on to share, "Kathy always gave 110 percent and was a go-getter. She looked at problems as challenges or opportunities and always took a proactive versus reactive point of view."

As a result, Kathy helped Jennifer "re-engage my passion for HR again and inspired me to want to continue my career in HR again. In previous roles, I was stuck in tactical, compliance, and mundane HR work. Kathy showcased how to drive results and make a positive difference on people and the business through her ability to be strategic and have a forward-thinking mindset."

From one stellar HR pro to another, you will remember Lauren Rudman. During a recent stop in her career of doing *HR Like a Boss,* she worked with Chris Schmitt, the vice president of strategic partnerships at the National Association of Manufacturers. Before that, Lauren and Chris worked together at ERICO.

Chris shared how Lauren successfully led a local, family-owned business through an acquisition by a much larger and very different organization: "The acquisition was a big culture shock, but thanks to my trust in Lauren, the transition was possible. She would say, 'You can trust me, I've got your back on this.' And that was just such a great way to experience a very emotional time in everyone's lives and careers, but also feeling like you had a friend who had their eye on the ball. We were only able to be successful with the folks from the plant and the folks from the organization as a whole, because they trusted Lauren as someone that they knew that they could rely on as a resource, but also somebody who wasn't going to come in and blow smoke at them."

Eda Erkal, who worked together with Erick Miles, came on my podcast to talk about Erick's amazingly awesome HR skills.

She explained that Erick "leads with curiosity. He wants to see any situation from all angles and he's *real.* I appreciate that about him because I know I'm going to get his HR perspective, which I don't always look through that lens, but I'm also getting a natural experienced person's support."

She went on to say,

> *He definitely makes himself available. I know that in a role like HR you have to wear many hats and he seemingly enjoys doing that, so it makes it easier. He's always available if I reach out and even if he's not available to me in the moment, there's always an acknowledgment. People just want to be seen, people just want to be heard, and he does that effort-lessly. Erick asks very strategic questions to really analyze the*

big picture and understand what's going on. He really gets into the root of a problem. He just exhibits that expertise, and it came naturally to him.

When I talked about thinking differently, I introduced you to Cindy Torres Essell. The impact she's had on numerous employees at Heinen's, including Jeff Berquist, is best summed up by Jeff's recounting:

Cindy is, herself, a true trusted advisor, and she's really helped me grow in my career, as a mentor and a friend. She gives us a lot of room to do our thing. And she has turned into more of a trusted advisor type role, where we'll keep her up to speed on things that are going on.

We know when to come to her for advice. She'll lend her perspective on where we need to be focusing our time and energy and maybe thinking about things differently, challenging us appropriately. It really has been a wonderful relationship as far as allowing us to grow and develop and at times to challenge us and get us to think differently when she feels it's warranted or needed. She's given me real confidence to do this role successfully. And I would argue one of the greatest tools she's ever taught me is being a trusted advisor myself. How to build relationships, how to be that consultant because in operations you're used to making the decisions.

We talked about my very own Steven Tyler: George Sample. George has been doing *HR Like a Boss* for a long time and ironically created his own personal mission statement to "make an impact" on as many people as he possibly could through his various roles in human resources. Talia Seals is one of those fortunate to have worked with George and learned from his employee-centric approach. Over the years, George and Talia have teamed up at various organizations and made a positive difference in each other's lives. Talia recalled the very first time she met George, and said, "He asked me right away about my HR network. I shared that I had been in a recruiting role for several years at a larger organization. Due to the demand of my role and high volume of work, I was not able to join SHRM. On day two of getting to know George, I was encouraged to join our local SHRM chapter along with getting a national SHRM membership. As a result, I have been able to make meaningful connections, build community, and give back to the HR profession."

George didn't stop there. Talia believed one of George's greatest strengths is his ability to give direct and candid feedback eloquently and effectively. She said, "By working with George, I learned the importance of connecting with employees beyond the mid-year and annual performance reviews. In watching George make himself available to everyone inside of our organization and building authentic connections with people, he is trusted by employees and is able to give feedback, hold people accountable, showcase their opportunities, and deliver heartfelt guidance. George's even-keeled approach and inquisitive nature have allowed him to develop meaningful relationships with countless people. As a result, he has advocated for so many people including those who may not feel they have a voice or are too timid to speak out."

Through delivering amazingly awesome HR, Talia went on to share, "George creates a sense of belonging within his team and the organization by valuing the opinions and strengths of others. As a result, the people that work for him are very loyal and never leave George. He gives individuals courage by finding their hidden talents and providing the needed space for innovation and creating new ideas. Out of that, I have seen progressive policies, improved procedures, and advanced marketing materials developed that drove results for our organization."

My hope in telling these stories is to inspire you to consider the immense impact you can have on someone's life. Many of the HR professionals I highlighted in this section were humbled and, at times, shocked by how little they felt they did that meant so much to someone else. To me, there is so much there for us to consider, and we should approach every single interaction that we have with a human being with tremendous care and consideration. You never know how your purpose-driven action can lead to making an impact.

Chapter 18
Recap

I think we all need to consider making work and life accommo-
dations that *advance* our business and relationship with our
employees. The "it's better for the company" approach is so 1990.
Employees work best and excel when they are aligned to a company's purpose, know what impact their role has on the business, and
understand how they fit into the team and culture. I'd recommend
looking through that lens when implementing any policy. To me,
having synergy between employees and your employer is the magic
sauce of success in this thing we call business.

The ideals of the human resources function are not a zero-sum
game. There won't always need to be winners and losers. Employees
can feel empowered, be engaged at work, and love what they do
while the company makes money and pays its employees, managers,
and leaders handsomely. When that harmony exists, the idea of business can transcend beyond the work that an employee does or the
product or service that a company produces or delivers. All of that
effort, strategy, and persistence can result in influential leaders and
successful companies making a positive difference in the community.
It is a trickle-down effect. Everyone benefits when the purposeful
outcome is carefully thought out and unified within an organization.

That said, human resources is not for everyone. It takes an
extraordinary person to do it well. HR is more than just working

with people; doing *HR Like a Boss* requires tremendous sacrifice, cutting into family time and personal aspirations. Not to mention, while dealing with people can bring immense joy, it can also cause added stress that can take a physical and mental toll on even the best of us.

So why do it? For me, it is the ability to impact peoples' lives. And how do you do that? I am so glad you ask.

To start, someone doing *HR Like a Boss* is a business leader first who just so happens to practice HR. Being a leader means taking responsibility for everything you do and owning your mindset, work, emotions, and effort. By having a leadership mindset, your perspective considers compliance and tactics, but also strategy and positive impacts. Leaders gain trust from everyone they work with, leading to respect because of their strategy and vision.

As you will recall, after taking ownership comes the idea of loving what you do and being passionate about it. This is a critical aspect in your journey toward being a boss. You cannot mail it in or simply just like helping people or growing your business. You must love what you do, who you work with, and the purpose of your company.

We are ready to conquer the world now that we have an own-it, love-it mindset. As a whole, the human resources community must think about its role and how it is done differently than they have in the past. It all starts with treating your job or department like it is your own business, which requires regularly investing time to think like a boss. Owners of a business do not make time or space for reasons or excuses but will instead seek various perspectives on what is the root cause of major issues. As an "owner" of your business, it is essential to understand every aspect of how the company you work for operates, from your organization's marketing of its brand to retaining its customers and everything in between. And, since growth and profitability are such critical pillars to business success, someone doing *HR Like a Boss* truly understands financial statements. With this knowledge, you can support your business and all of its employees while knowing how your organization does and does *not* make money. The final aspect of thinking differently is all about improving and leveraging your emotional intelligence to model behaviors to your team and all your employees, showing them how to use their emotions wisely and be an emotion scientist for themselves and others.

Now that our mindset focuses on collaborating and looking at your role differently, it is time to start being different. It is no longer about how much you know in your specialty or discipline as your expertise is assumed. Those that do *HR Like a Boss* do not stay complacent, are always growing their HR and business knowledge, and are intensely focused on consistently doing their job well. In order to do so, you must seek feedback from everyone around you to improve yourself and your employees and drive results for your organization. One critical aspect of being different is your ability to leverage technology. By doing so, you can allow your HR system to take on some of the mundane but necessary tactics so you don't get distracted and can focus on bigger and better aspects of your role and responsibilities.

It's not enough to just be different. To truly be different, we must be better at what we do every moment, day, and in every interaction with our employees. Just like we see with our favorite sports team, our organizations need to acquire exceptional new talent while developing those already on our squad. One of the first places to start is to ensure your managers have the proper skills, abilities, and mindset to develop their teams. Providing clarity and communicating consistently are the foundation for success in ensuring managers display these qualities. Along the way, situations will arise without a clear policy in place or that cannot be found in your employee handbook. Someone doing *HR Like a Boss* examines the facts, trusts their gut, and can make tough decisions. As a result of this approach, you will develop meaningful and lasting relationships that will transcend your work.

Strategic Business Plan Components

One of the key aspects of being better at what you do is taking action. To act like someone doing *HR Like a Boss*, we need a well-thought-out plan that we operationalize like a boss. The *HR Like a Boss* plan includes a keen focus on five key pillars:

1. Having a purposeful commitment,
2. Being people centric,
3. Helping your people produce consistently,
4. Having continuity amongst all of your key processes, and
5. Understanding your profitable components.

Last but certainly not least in your journey of achieving amazingly awesome HR is your ability to make a meaningful impact on your colleagues' and employees' lives. You can strive to go even one step further, ensuring that your organization is making a positive difference in your community.

Wow, that is a lot. As I mentioned before, HR is not for the faint of heart, especially for someone who wants to stand out and be a leader.

Speaking of leaders, we are going to end *HR Like a Boss* with these steps to take to start delivering amazingly awesome HR immediately.

Go "All In"

First, to reach beyond your current state, you must be "all in." You cannot partially be into HR or just simply like working with people. You must love what you do every day and be inspired by helping others. Why? Because there are a ton of crappy things that you are going to face daily that can easily set you off course. If you love what you do, you know it. You look forward to working every day and understanding your purpose in the grand scheme of things.

On the flipside, if you truly do not love what you are doing, then it is time to have a heart-to-heart with yourself about what you love to do. Dig into what you have a passion for. Be honest with yourself. Stop faking it. Don't beat yourself up because HR is not the right fit for you. It is okay. People change. Priorities shift. You have evolved.

If you are really "all in," no one has to tell you what to do. You just do it. Having this type of ownership mentality will ensure you keep your eye on the prize and persevere through the most challenging situations. You are working every day to get a little better than the day before.

Is Your CEO Down with HR?

The next step is to ensure you have a CEO who is truly passionate about people and sees value in the human resources function. Without the CEO's support, you will feel like Sisyphus every single workday. The simplest way to measure a CEO's commitment to HR boils down to three key points:

1. The human resources leader of your organization sits on the executive team, and the CEO regularly counsels the head of HR about a wide array of business- and people-related challenges and opportunities.
2. The CEO has an affinity for the company's employees and there is a direct correlation between the importance of doing the right thing for employees and efforts to achieve business success. In other words, the CEO's actions must match their words when it comes to the importance of their employees. If the company's employees are sincerely the top priority of the organization, then you are golden.
3. Your CEO understands that a strategic business plan should balance people, purpose, and profit, and genuinely lives by these values.

If you do not happen to have a supportive CEO who values HR, I would strongly encourage you to speak with your other HR colleagues to understand what is causing the disconnect. Once you have that information, put the full-court press on your *HR Like a Boss* plan and implement it in everything you do. Gauge the reaction of your executive leadership, especially your CEO. If your actions are not getting noticed, or worse, people are questioning your amazingly awesome efforts, it may be time to start looking for another gig. There is no sense beating your head against a wall if your CEO and senior leadership are not down with your effort to drive results from amazingly awesome HR. Once you find that right next opportunity where HR is supported top-down, let your HR colleagues and even your CEO know exactly why you left (as always, be clear and kind).

Be Insatiable About Strategy

Over the years, developing my personal approach to being strategic has been a long and, at times, elusive road. As someone who thrived on action, I struggled in the past to make time for strategic thinking. However, life experience, wisdom from others, and simplifying the concept clarified how to *be strategic*. Here are my simple suggestions for being more strategic:

> *Stop and think.* We have mentioned this idea a few times in the book. Have you ever gotten lost while traveling? What did you do? Continue to aimlessly drive around town? Or did you stop your car, check out Google Maps, confirm the address you are going to, then start on this corrected path? If you feel like you are adrift in your career or things are out of control, take the time to think about what is going on, why it is happening, and what options you have to make it better. On the other hand, if you have momentum in what you are doing, play to your strengths and leverage to make a significant change.

> *Simplify strategy.* Strategic thinking boils down to reiterating two simple questions. For your personal life, it comes down to, How am I different? How can I be better? Organizationally, we

look at those same two questions but framed for your organization: How is the company different? How can we be better? The first part of this book was all about taking a strategic view on how to achieve amazingly awesome HR. In order to make things better or improve your situation, you have to understand where you are and where you want to be. Then, you understand the gap that exists, and you attack it.

Build It and They Will Come

Previous chapters outlined the key steps to consider when building your plan for doing *HR Like a Boss*. We looked at the necessary components to build your strategic business plan, which used a formula that balanced purposeful commitment, people-centric values, and profit components, and then rounded out your plan with process continuity, consistent production, and personal characteristics. Many of the greatest personal and professional achievements our world has seen have been a result of a well-thought-out plan being executed to perfection. Although we do not expect perfection, someone doing *HR Like a Boss* strives to get a little bit better every day. Having a plan about what you are trying to improve and why you are doing it in the first place will drastically increase your chances of achieving whatever you set out to do.

Wax On–Wax Off

Of course, we use another eighties reference to bring home the final step in making amazingly awesome HR a reality. Remember Ralph Macchio's character, Daniel LaRusso, in *Karate Kid* getting scolded repeatedly by Mr. Miyagi to beat the hated crew from Cobra Kai. Mr. Miyagi's famous wax on, wax off reference caused Daniel LaRusso to master one of the key karate moves and the rest is history. Mastering what you do only seems fitting to me, especially if we are going to spend such a significant part of our life working. We might as well become damn good at it. Here are a few suggestions to advance your HR skills and develop a command of what you do like a boss:

» *Hire a coach.* Daniel LaRusso was just a random kid before he met Mr. Miyagi. The right coach will change your life forever.
» *Be an insatiable learner.* Whether reading a book from a thought leader you admire or subscribing to your idol's podcast, you can learn so much by listening to what experts with decades of experience have to say.
» *Make it iterative.* Honing your craft and making continuous improvements will drive improvements. At the same time, strive to avoid complacency like the plague. To make this easy, focus on one key aspect of improvement every quarter to make sure you progress on at least one major personal or professional goal.
» *Turn your EQ into a superpower.* The most successful people I know in business and life have found a way to leverage their emotional intelligence. It gives them an advantage in almost every situation they face in their lives.
» *Build a community.* Surround yourself with other like-minded people that fill you up with positive, motivating energy. Having a community of trusted advisors, colleagues, and friends who hold themselves to a high standard can only make you better at what you do.

The Journey Starts Today

This brings us to the end of the book, but the journey is never over. What you do with my opinions in the book and the stories from countless business leaders who are rocking it and making a difference with their employees, company, and community is completely up to you. I hope that my words and the stories of real people doing amazingly awesome HR inspire you to take your game to another level.

If you are looking for additional support and resources, please check out www.hrlikeaboss.com for tools, tips, online courses, inclusive community, podcasts, blogs, workbooks, and a wide array of tricks to help you think differently, be different, be better, take action, and make an impact. In addition, the website will help you find ways to connect with other HR professionals who already do or are inspired to do *HR Like a Boss*.

Last but not least, I am here to help you in any way that I can. No matter your request, please reach out to me via john@willory.com. I would love to hear from you about how much you loved or hated (and anything in between) the book, what you think about the resources at www.hrlikeaboss.com, your personal journey in the business world and HR field, a story that made a positive impact on your employees, company, or community, or how a colleague show-cases doing *HR Like a Boss*.

Until next time, let's continue to aspire to do amazingly awesome HR!

References

Adler, Lou. "Here Are the Best (and Worst) Predictors of Quality of Hire." LinkedIn. *Talent Blog*, January 11, 2018. https://www.linkedin.com/business/talent/blog/talent-analytics/most-important-predictors-of-quality-of-hire.

Anspaugh, David, dir. *Hoosiers. 1986.*

Brackett, Marc. *Permission to Feel: Unlock the Power of Emotions to Help Our Kids, Ourselves, and Our Society Thrive.* London: Quercus Publishing, 2019.

Byham, Tacy, and Richard Wellins. *Your First Leadership Job: How Catalyst Leaders Bring Out the Best in Others.* Hoboken, NJ: Wiley, 2015.

Cambridge Dictionary. s.v. "human resources (n.)." Accessed April 4, 2023. https://dictionary.cambridge.org/us/dictionary/english/human-resources.

Cardon, Melissa S., Joakim Wincent, Jagdip Singh, and Mateja Drnovsek. "The Nature and Experience of Entrepreneurial Passion." *Academy of Management* 34, no. 3 (2009): 517. https://doi.org/10.5465/amr.2009.40633190.

Carnegie, Dale. *How to Win Friends and Influence People.* New York: Simon & Schuster, 2009. First published 1936.

Clear, James. *Atomic Habits: Tiny Changes, Remarkable Results; An Easy & Proven Way to Build Good Habits & Break Bad Ones.* New York: Avery, 2018.

Development Dimensions International. *The Frontline Leader Project: Exploring the Most Critical Segment of Leaders.* DDI, 2019. https://media.ddiworld.com/ebooks/FLL-eBook-interactive.pdf.

Dictionary.com. s.v. "like a boss." Accessed April 14, 2023. https://www.dictionary.com/e/slang/like-a-boss/.

Dooney, John. *Workforce Analytics: Critical Evaluation of How Organizational Staff Size Influences HR Metrics.* SHRM, 2015.

Dictionary.com. s.v. "like a boss." Accessed April 14, 2023. https://www.dictionary.com/e/slang/like-a-boss/.

"Dr. Marc Brackett and Brené on 'Permission to Feel.'" Interview by Brené Brown. Unlocking Us, April 2020. https://brenebrown.com/podcast/dr-marc-brackett-and-brene-on-permission-to-feel/.

Dweck, Carol S. *Mindset: The New Psychology of Success*, reprint edition. New York, NY: Ballantine Books, 2007.

Ferrazzi, Keith and Tahl Raz. *Never Eat Alone: And Other Secrets to Success, One Relationship at a Time.* New York: Crown Business, 2005.

Fisk, Peter. "Why Do Purpose-Driven Companies Do Better?" LinkedIn, February 1, 2019. https://www.linkedin.com/pulse/why-do-purpose-driven-companies-better-peter-fisk.

Goulston, Mark. *Just Listen: Discover the Secret to Getting Through to Absolutely Anyone.* New York: American Management Association, 2010.

"Need a Quick Brain Boost? Take a Walk." *Harvard Health*, July 14, 2016. https://www.health.harvard.edu/mind-and-mood/need-a-quick-brain-boost-take-a-walk.

Patterson, Kerry, Joseph Grenny, Ron McMillan, and Al Switzler. *Crucial Accountability: Tools for Resolving Violated Expectations, Broken Commitments, and Bad Behavior*. Maidenhead, England: McGraw-Hill, 2013.

Patterson, Kerry, Joseph Grenny, Ron McMillan, and Al Switzler. *Crucial Conversations: Tools for Talking When Stakes Are High*. Maidenhead, England: McGraw-Hill, 2012.

Ruiz, Don Miguel. *The Four Agreements*. San Rafael, CA: Amber-Allen Publishing, 1997.

Stein, Alan, Jr. "Kobe Bryant's Insane Obsession with the Basics." YouTube, March 25, 2020. https://www.youtube.com/watch?v=RYtUq8a5Er8.

Urban Dictionary. s.v. "Like a boss." Accessed April 14, 2023. https://www.urbandictionary.com/define.php?term=Like+a+boss.

Wilkie, Dana. "Do Your Employees Hate HR?" SHRM, February 5, 2016. https://www.shrm.org/resourcesandtools/hr-topics/employee-relations/pages/hr-success-stories.aspx.

Index

About the Author

John is a husband, father, brother, entrepreneur, and lifelong Northeast Ohioan. He has been married to his wife, Emily, for twenty-five years. He is the proud father of Will and Mallory. John was an Academic All-American in golf at Kent State University and began his professional career at ADP.

Over the last twenty years, he has started or been an owner in six ventures. He currently is the president and founder of Willory, a staffing and consulting firm focused on HR & payroll. The firm helps clients find top talent for HR & payroll direct hire and temporary roles along with providing HR & payroll advisory and HR technology consulting services. In addition, John is the majority owner of Centsible Water, Ohio's premier reverse osmosis water vending company. As well, he partnered to help start the first ever fractional sales management, sales training, and sales search firm, Keylan Management Group.

John is a keynote speaker and consistently dazzles attendees with the positive business impact that HR can have on employees, businesses, and communities. He has spoken at hundreds of events and conferences. You can find John on his weekly podcast, *HR Like a Boss*, available on all popular podcast platforms.

John loves to golf, coach sports, and root for Cleveland sports teams.